Maria's Story

Maria's Story

by Robin Barratt
with Inna Barratt

Diverse Publishing Ltd

First Published in April 2005 by Diverse Publishing Ltd

ISBN 0 9548143 1 2

Typeset in 11/13pt Sabon
by e-type, Liverpool

Printed and bound in Great Britain by
Cox and Wyman Ltd, Reading, Berkshire

Diverse Publishing Ltd
37 Binfield Rd, Bracknell, Berkshire, RG42 2AW, Great Britain
Tel: 0870 240 9998
www.diversepublishing.com
sales@diversepublishing.com

About the Author

Although Robin Barratt still runs the membership department of the Worldwide Federation of Bodyguards, he has all but given up bodyguarding. Robin is now an author and freelance writer, amongst other things edits *PROTECTION News* magazine, the only magazine in the world dedicated to close protection. He is a member of the National Union of Journalists, his first book, *Doing the Doors* is an honest account of his life as a bodyguard and doorman in the pubs and clubs around the UK.

Author's note:

This story is based on actual events as they happened between spring 2003 and the present day.

Part Two – "Maria's Story" is a true story based around Maria's life as told by Maria herself in a meeting one day in the spring of 2003. In some cases names have been invented or changed and situations slightly altered to suit the format of the book.

Part Three – "Walking Tall" are actual events and discussions as they took place from October 2003 to the present day. Only slight editing had been made to the spelling in some of the e-mails.

Contents

This book is dedicated to my wonderful daughter Daniella, I love you...

Prologue

Sitting down on that eventful day in Moscow over two years ago listening to Maria tell her story has changed my life forever. I suppose, if I could do anything in the world apart from writing, I would set up a facility in Moscow helping the disabled and destitute. In a small way my wife Inna and I have started to transform Maria and her son's life, but Maria has given us so much more. She has made me recognise something in me I felt I knew I had, but never really had any chance of developing.

Most of us do want to help and a lot of us occasionally pop a coin into the bucket, never really getting involved, not really emotional, caring just enough to give that pound but then walking away without any concern or another thought. I was the same – rarely giving and caring little. However, involving myself with Maria and her young son and striving to fulfil the promises we made to her, has eternally changed me. I now understand the hope we give with our promises and the sadness and despair we witness when those promises are not realised.

Maria has experienced more in her short life than most of us will ever experience. For the most part Maria's life has been awful, but amazingly she still retains a scale of hope and aspiration that continues to astonish and surprise. Maria dreams of a better life – she dreams of being a better mother, a mother her son will one day look up to and admire.

If this book does nothing else, it should give us all hope and make us realise that, no matter how hard or how bad life gets, there is always a way out, there are always chances and opportunities and there are always people around us that really do care.

Firstly and unconventionally Inna and I have to thank everyone that called, wrote and e-mailed with their *false* promises to help. Some people promised so many things but ended up giving nothing and we never heard from them again. Those false promises motivated us to work even harder. With her initial telephone call Heather Mills-McCartney promised us, and more importantly Maria, so much and yet at the time of writing this book and almost two years later has actually done very little. For an incredibly wealthy woman who has, in some ways, lived a similar life to Maria, this saddened and disappointed us beyond belief. This story not only chronicles Maria's amazing life and the incredible effort everyone made in getting her walking again, but also our fight to make Heather fulfil the initial promises she made.

Secondly, and infinitely more importantly, we have to thank everyone that pledged their support and who actually helped us in ways we still find hard to believe. Without the help from the Icelandic prosthetic company Össur, we would never have had new legs for Maria, enabling Maria to actually take that first giant step, both physically and mentally, towards a new life. And of course we have to thank Jamie Gillespie, the British prosthetist who works for Össur and who went over to Moscow time and time again to work with Maria. And of course a big thank you goes to Andrei and their clinic in Moscow who worked so hard. You all gave us the inspiration and determination to succeed.

We must also thank those who have given money to Maria to make life for her and her son a little more comfortable including Tim, Allan and the staff at CIA Excel Risk Consultancy, Mrs. Hingley, Mrs Loveday, Mrs Mitchell, Mrs J E Bruce, The Norwich Russian Group, Mr. G Tilsley, A J Howe, Mr Mann, J Ogden, Mrs M Heald, David & Barbara Herman, Jim Beaumont, S P Vassallo, J H Delaney, Mrs J Hammond, S A Milligan, Ms Illingworth, Sarah Baker, James Howells, S M Harris, Mr Cooper, Mr Eley, Ms Jeary, Master G Baker and the staff at Norwich Union as well as the other anonymous donations we received. It truly amazed and moved us how much everyone actually genuinely cared about Maria and her son.

In a country with little or no state support Maria sadly still begs to survive. At the time of writing, she still goes out every day to her miserable corner in the dirty Metro, on her small wooden platform and pleads to passers-by for help. Sadly, as this book went into print, we heard that Maria had spent ten days in hospital after being beaten up so our priority now is to get Maria off the streets. If you can help in any way please contact us – our details and the details of the Foundation we have set up to help Maria and others like her can be found at the back of the book.

Not only does this book record Maria's tragic and harsh life on the streets of Moscow but it aims to give inspiration and hope to others like Maria, as well as recording the astonishing care that people have felt for her and her son. We also hope that the Russian government might one day look at its draconian attitude to care and support for its disabled population and enforce the laws that it occasionally and half heartily makes. Healthcare in Russia is still free but the money that the Russian government allocates to the disabled disappears into the pockets of the officials allocating it long before it ever reaches its destination. Yet the Government actively frowns upon and discourages foreign aid and charities. The Russian government cannot and does not want to look after its disabled and destitute, nor does it want anyone else to – being disabled in Russia is being a prisoner in your home, with your only destiny the four walls that surround you.

Robin Barratt

PART ONE

Finding Maria

Winters in Moscow are long, harsh and hard. Temperatures often drop from between minus twenty and minus thirty, and on occasions even lower. I looked outside at the falling snow and understood how much I really do hate the Russian winters. I hate going out – having to dress in so many layers and yet still feel cold. I hate wearing thick gloves, thick hat and a scarf covering my mouth – the taste of bits of wool mixed with condensation always makes me feel like vomiting. I hate the blind trudge through the thick snow, my head and body huddled against the driving blizzards. I hate queuing up for the number seventeen minibus, which stops opposite the supermarket not far from my apartment, waiting quietly and patiently until the bus pulls up and then the mad frenzy as everyone surges forward and battles to find a place to stand (there are rarely any seats). Old frail looking grandmothers, smiling sweetly and chatting happily about their grandchildren are suddenly transformed into merciless warriors as they fight and push and claw their way on. Everyone follows suit – no one wants to spend another fifteen minutes standing in the snow and relentless, biting cold – if you weren't willing to fight your way onto the bus and into a space, even before the bus has fully stopped, you would be probably be standing freezing at the bus stop for hours. One evening I remember having to walk home in the driving rain as, even after the third attempt, I still didn't manage to get myself onto a bus. I was pulled back and pushed aside time and time again until I simply gave up. There were no taxis, so I walked the two miles home in the cold and pouring rain, moaning, extremely bad-tempered and wishing I was some place else.

Once on the bus, things don't get much better. Minibuses that are made to carry fifteen passengers often have double that amount squeezed on. Money for the fare is passed down the bus from passenger to passenger, eventually making its way to the driver who precariously sorts out the fares and change while recklessly negotiating and manoeuvring through the traffic, often at break-neck speed. Condensation in the minibuses is so thick it is virtually impossible to see out the windows and therefore to know when to get off. The driver will only stop when requested, miss the stop and off you go to the next and another long walk back in the snow. Normal buses are less frequent than minibuses but are twice as full. Even with relative warmth of a full bus, icicles hang from the ceiling and the floor as slippery as an ice rink.

I walked over to the window and looked at the thermometer: minus twenty four. My journey to the other side of Moscow to meet Inna, my wife, was not going to be pleasant. I wasn't looking forward to it in the slightest. I looked down at my watch, it was three o'clock in the afternoon and I had two hours to get ready and get myself across Moscow to a typically Russian bistro that we had arranged to meet at near to her office. Called "Moo- Moo" it served tasty, hot and very cheap Russian cuisine in a large self-service restaurant packed with noisy Russians eating before their inevitable long, cold journey home.

I looked down to the streets below, at the few huddled figures rushing here and there. It was snowing heavily, horribly cold and no one in their right mind would ever spend any longer outside than absolutely necessary. Any part of the body left uncovered would, within a few short minutes, be stinging and raw and painful. No Russian would ever dream about going outside in mid winter without layers of heavy clothing, a thick, furry, warm hat, thick boots and heavy insulated gloves. When I first came to Moscow I had the misfortune of forgetting, or perhaps not thinking I would need a hat. As I left the apartment I wondered why those around me looked both horrified and concerned. Within a few short minutes of being outside I completely understood – my head was thumping with the intense cold and my ears burned. It was minus thirty two that day and I had no choice but to turn around and quickly go back home. It can sometimes be so cold that the water in your eyes would actually start to freeze, and I have even had a bottle of vodka turn to thick syrup after just a short walk from the supermarket to my apartment. Russian winters are unforgiving.

I knew it would take me about an hour to get to the restaurant. I had a ten minute walk to the bus stop – I was really hoping I wouldn't have to wait too long for a bus – then a ten minute bus journey to the nearest Metro station at Prospect Vernadskogo. From Prospect Vernadskogo I would then take the Metro into the centre of Moscow, changing lines at Chistye Prudy station, to Alekseevskaya, my destination. Thankfully "Moo-Moo", with its large black and white sign of a Friesian cow outside, was just next to the Metro at Alekseevskaya and just a two minute walk.

My wife took this journey every morning and every night, five days a week, and in every kind of weather. I was reluctant to do it just the once. I hadn't been outside in almost a week, preferring the solitude of the computer and my thoughts about the couple of articles I had been contracted to write about Russian life for British magazines.

I had originally come to Moscow as a bodyguard for a chairman of a multi-national company. This was how I met

Inna. She was working for the security company I worked in partnership with. Whenever I needed Russian bodyguards, or run an investigation for a western company with interests in Russia, I would always call her. She was the personal assistant to the ex KGB Director and had contacts for almost anything. After a few months of speaking to her on the telephone and occasionally popping into their office, I asked her out.

Bodyguarding and security had been my life since the late eighties, and I have travelled the world protecting the rich and famous. I tended to concentrate primarily on areas of high risk, and had spent time in Bosnia during the conflict, Israel, Africa and Asia, but as I got older the appeal and excitement grew less and my safety and the future of my daughter became the most important thing. Although I didn't see her that often I would speak to her every few days, write once a week and see her whenever I could. I didn't want her to grow up with just a picture of me on the mantlepiece, knowing that her Daddy got killed in some far off place protecting someone she never heard of. I had more or less given up bodyguarding. I had taken a journalist course, joined the National Union of Journalist and now made my frugal living in Moscow as a freelance writer writing stories and selling them. I had written about the difficulties of being black in Moscow, the prejudice, the hatred, the beatings. This won an award from IMPACT Magazine. I had also written about two gay women struggling with their sexuality in society where being gay was, until just a few years ago, a criminal offence. I enjoyed writing and had just finished my first book. One of the articles I had been contracted to write was about a female bodyguard protecting her client against the Russian mafia, which I found fascinating. I really did not want to go out but I had promised Inna I would meet her that evening and buy her dinner and so, reluctantly, I searched for my boots, hat, scarf and gloves.

With my mind focused on a large steaming bowl of Borsch soup, I locked the apartment door and called for the elevator. As I waited for the antiquated lift to slowly make its way from the 22nd floor to the 6th, I could feel myself getting hotter and hotter. That was another thing I remembered I hated about the Russian winters – wearing layers and layers of clothing for the outside, and then having to get on the packed, hot, stuffy Metro, wrapped up and insulated against the bitter cold outside. You quickly feel like being slowly baked inside a microwave. After a few short minutes it becomes unbearable and you crave to at least take your coat off. But there is generally no room and you stand and sweat and suffer. For me the worst bit was not the baking but the going back outside into the freezing cold with sweat running down my back.

Going from plus twenty to minus twenty in one swing of a door never fails to shock me. Almost all apartment blocks in Moscow are communally heated twenty four hours a day throughout the winter. Big industrial boilers feed large areas of high rise apartment blocks day in day out – there is no individual temperature control, heating is either on or off. In the summer heating is off, in the winter it is on and in the height of the winter the temperature inside the apartment blocks is probably around twenty degrees. Twenty four hour heating and hot water for a tiny monthly fee is one of the slightly better things about living through a Russian winter, rarely did my monthly utility bill exceed ten pounds. But walking from plus twenty into minus twenty is like being slammed full on by a speeding truck. The cold hits you hard and it takes a few moments to catch your breath. Breathing through the mouth is dangerous and can quickly freeze the moisture that lines the throat, so you have to slowly inhale through your nose and exhale through your mouth. After a few slow breaths, and a lot more grumbles, I pulled my hat lower over my ears, pulled my coat collar higher and trundled as quickly as I could towards the bus-stop.

Even though I did indeed hate the Russian winters and longed for the sun and the summer, there is something truly magical about the snow. I can honestly say that Moscow city centre – the Red Square and Kremlin, on a bright sunny morning after a thick layer of fresh snow, is one of the most beautiful and magical looking places in the world. The irony is of a fairytale, innocent, magical looking palace inhabited by ruthless, authoritarian dictators.

We lived in quite a nice area of Moscow, south of the city centre, not far from the university, where many lecturers, teachers and academics lived. By British standards the rows and rows of high rise apartment blocks would have long ago been marked for demolition and, admittedly, in the autumn rain and spring thaw the place looks deprived and dirty and impoverished, but in the snow the whole area has a perfect, clean, healthy feel. It is as though, for a few months of every year, everything that is dirty and corrupt and immoral about Russia is covered by a sheet of clean, white, crispy linen. When it first starts to snow everything is beautiful and exciting and different, but after a few months of unremitting cold and relentless driving snow, it is no-longer nice, everything is bad and horrible and depression and despair settles in.

Thankfully, going into Moscow at that time in the afternoon is not nearly as hectic as early in the morning and a minibus was waiting at the bus-stop. Only half full, I clambered on, paid the driver the seven roubles (fifteen pence) fare and found a seat at the back. Late morning and early afternoon minibuses have a tendency to wait until they are almost full before setting off. This is great if you are at the beginning of the route, which thankfully I was, but not so good if you live midway along a route as then, generally, the minibuses are completely full and speedily pass waiting passengers. A couple of passengers quickly followed me onboard, slamming the sliding door behind them. The driver crunched the minibus into first gear and we started to move.

Almost all Russian minibuses are old and dilapidated and have had years of abuse, and DIY botched repairs. Together with the appalling state of many Moscow roads, most journeys, however short, are incredibly uncomfortable. The suspension on most minibuses simply does not exist, thumping through and bouncing over the dozens of potholes that litter most routes causes you to tightly grip the seat rail in front and hold on for all your worth. Engines snarl and roar and sound as though it would be the minibus' last kilometre, ever. Gears scrape and crunch, handbrakes almost never work and no one has ever heard of a catalytic converter. Taking a Russian minibus is not for the fainthearted and almost no foreigner, ever, takes a minibus anywhere. If I had a choice nor would I, but I didn't have a car and there was no other way, apart from a long walk, to the nearest Metro.

I suffered in silence as the minibus rattled and rocked its way to Prospect Vernadskogo Metro station. Thankfully most minibuses stop at the Metro stations without being requested. I got off with almost all the other passengers and followed the trail of huddled bodies down the steps into the Moscow Metro system – probably one of the best and most efficient underground systems in the world.

Unlike the London underground, where annoying neon signs inform you that the next train to Ealing Broadway would be in approximately five days time, the Moscow Metro trains run without fail every two or three minutes. The cost of ten Metro tickets is fifty roubles (about one pound), which is about ten pence a ride to anywhere in Moscow. Whether you are going one stop, or from one end of Moscow to the other, one ride is just ten pence. Whenever

I returned to London I would always be horrified at the cost, the inefficiency and the crazy zone system of the London underground. As with many things in England, the underground is extremely expensive and exceedingly unreliable. Not so in Moscow – the Metro, when it isn't particularly crowded, is a wonder of technology. Not only that, many of the Metro stations are simply awesome. Brilliantly designed, beautifully decorated and wonderfully kept, the Moscow Metro system is a stunning tourist attraction by itself and can be ranked alongside The Red Square, The Kremlin and The Bolshoi.

I bought my block of ten tickets from the sorrowful looking cashier, passed one of the many thousands of Moscow's wretched beggars, standing silently with head bowed and an outstretched grubby hand holding a few miserable kopeks (100 kopeks = 1 rouble), and boarded the train that had just pulled in. After a while you don't even notice the beggars – their faces and their despair. Another one of a thousand, maybe two thousand, it is impossible to give to everyone so I didn't give to any. I quickly walked passed them all, trying not to look at their faces, not even considering that they were human and suffering terribly. After the first few weeks living in a world of poverty and deprivation, I became so accustomed to beggars on every street corner, in every Metro station, outside every supermarket – to me they no longer existed. There were not drug addicts, alcoholics or mentally ill but soldiers whose legs had been blown off in Chechnya, or men and women old enough to be my grandparents, or those unfortunately born disabled or facially disfigured, or the destitute – Moscow was full of them, all unable to survive in a normal world and all on the streets begging for survival. They were all begging for their next hot meal – *not* for their next fix or bottle of meths.

I hated myself for walking past, for not even looking at them but I knew I had neither the money nor the ability to help. What could I do? I often imagined myself a multi-millionaire paying someone to travel the Metro system day in day out handing out enough money for a hot meal and better clothing to every beggar they would come across. Or perhaps setting up a sanctuary where the destitute, the disabled and the elderly could get warm and eat a good meal. I completely understood that this really wasn't the answer – giving like this would never ever be enough, but surely it would give someone, somewhere a little comfort, even for a day? I so wanted to do something for these people, they were not addicts or ill, but normal people blighted by Russia's corruption.

Being the second biggest oil producer in the world, Russia should be one of the wealthiest countries in the world, but greed is colossal and most of the money the Russian government allocates to the poor and needy never reaches them. It is filtered away down the bureaucratic line into the pockets of everyone but those that need it the most. There are very few Russian charities in Russia, no one really cares for or bothers about anyone else apart from themselves. No one trusts the banks, the government, the police, the system and everyone's preoccupation is surviving themselves, protecting their own wealth. No one gives to Russian charities as they believe, and often rightly so, that the money will not go to the cause but into the pockets of the charity directors. There is little accountability and an enormous amount of corruption and crime. As a westerner with different morals and ethics I was shocked to the core when I saw an ambulance, lights flashing, siren screaming, struggling to get through a queue of traffic. No one moved. The ambulance just sat there in traffic and no one cared. This, for me, summed up Russia's attitude to others – they just don't care. There is no country anywhere else in the world whose inhabitants ignore the cries of the ambulance. I remembered an interesting documentary on Russian television, which Inna translated for me. It concerned a newly married couple who sat in their car in front of an ambulance, ignoring its sirens and flashing lights and continuous banging of the horn. They were in traffic on their way home and didn't want to lose their place in the queue. They refused to move or to let the ambulance pass, all the way back to their apartment block they sat in slow moving traffic directly in front of the ambulance. Just as they turned up outside their apartment, the woman's mother rushed to meet the ambulance, crying and screaming as to why the ambulance had taken so long. The ambulance was visiting that same couple's son who had suddenly fallen critically ill.

There are, of course, a few charities operating in Russia, mainly foreign and few and far between. These are generally frowned upon by the Russian government. The Russian government still does not like foreign aid – it is an old communist mind-set that Russia and its people are too proud to accept help from others. They believe they should support their own, even though they won't and don't and that most of the money is stolen by the same people that originally allocated it.

With the huge amount of resources coming from oil production, Russia should have the best hospitals and health care, the best schools, the best pensions and infrastructure in the world. But they have the worst because no one cares for anyone and the huge amount of wealth is quickly siphoned away and stolen.

And so the streets are littered with beggars and the destitute and I, along with most others, walk quickly past, head bowed, fiddling with my Metro ticket or pretending to make a mobile phone call.

The Metro from Prospect Vernadskogo to Chistye Prudy wasn't that busy, most people at that time of the afternoon were travelling out from the city centre, but from Chistye

Prudy leaving the city to Alekseevskaya, I knew the Metro was going to be packed. I managed to find a seat, took off my thick gloves, took out my mobile phone and started to text Inna telling her I was on my way. There was no signal but we would soon be travelling for a short time above ground over the Moskva River and I would press the "send" button as we stopped at the new Vorobyovy Gory station. The first stop after Prospect Vernadskogo was Universitet (Moscow State University). I knew the route well by now and sat huddled over the phone, typing my text. I vaguely heard the recording informing us that the doors were closing and the next stop was Vorobyovy Gory, and felt the train start to move. I didn't look up. No one looks up once they have found a seat. They engross themselves in a book, or play with their phone, or pretend to sleep – anything but look up. If they looked up they might see an elderly frail passenger, gripping the rail, struggling to support themselves as the carriage rocked backwards and forwards, and no one wants to give up their seat.

I was the same. It was a long journey and seats were rare and, even though I was relatively young and fit, I didn't fancy standing for the whole journey. I kept myself pre-occupied with my phone, staring at it hoping no one needed a seat. I had been in Moscow six months and was behaving like the Russians, struggling to survive and only thinking about myself.

A few seconds after the train has pulled away from the platform I felt the presence of someone standing directly in front of me. I didn't want to look up but somehow felt compelled to see who it was that was so close and invading my personal space.

"Pa-a-da-a-y-te na pro-pi-ta-a-nie." (Please, give me a few roubles for food).

Reluctantly I looked up to see a man of about thirty years old looking down at me. He had fairly short mousey coloured hair, was clean shaven with about a three inch scar diagonally running across his chin. His face appeared quite kind, but his eyes looked sad and distressed and vacant, as though he knew this was his empty, heartless miserable destiny. He wore a white, torn and slightly soiled vest and out from each side of his vest were two short stumps where his arms should have been. The right stump ended just above the elbow, the left a couple of inches below his shoulder. There were jagged scars on each stump – he was not disabled because of an abnormality at birth but from an accident, probably while in the army and probably, considering his age and the fact that he wore combat trousers, from the war in Chechnya.

He smiled and looked down and nodded at a small bag hanging from his neck. "Pa-a-da-a-y-te na pro-pi-ta-a-nie."

I wanted to know what had happened to him and how he survived those horrific injuries. What kind of life was he living? Where did he go once his day's begging had ended? How long had he been begging on the Metro like this and who looked after him? Did he have a family, children, wife, mother, father? What drove him to travel the dirty Metro every day begging to survive? Was there nothing else he could do? I thought about all the hundreds of beggars I have seen on Moscow's streets, all with a story to tell, all leading such miserable, desolate lives, all struggling to survive. Every day, day in day out, they stand and beg and hope for mercy but every day no mercy comes, their lives never change, their destiny remains exactly the same.

I rummaged in my pocket for some change and placed it into his small bag. He nodded, said "Spasiba" (thank you) and moved on down the carriage saying the same thing to the other passengers. I watched as most of the passengers in my carriage remained with their heads bowed pre-occupied with their books or pretending to sleep, not looking up, not acknowledging this desperate human being standing in front of them. The few passengers that did look up said no and quickly looked down again. He wouldn't plead, he just moved onto the next person and the next and the next, making his way slowly down the carriage. As the train stopped at the station he jumped off, walked down the platform and jumped back on at the next carriage. I looked through the murky glass windows of the carriage's connecting doors and could just about make out his unusual shape as he made his way down that carriage. This was his life, jumping from carriage to carriage displaying his disability in the hope of just enough sympathy to buy his next meal.

Change!! I felt disgusted and horrified with myself. Change!! I probably only gave him fifteen roubles, about thirty pence. Why didn't I give more? I could afford to have given him a lot more. Why was I so afraid of giving? Why didn't I give him one hundred or two hundred roubles? I had the money in my wallet. My excuse to myself was that if I gave him a hundred roubles, I would have to give every beggar a hundred roubles, but I didn't give to anyone anyway. Why did I feel resentment at giving when I knew there was no alternative for people like him? Unlike England, Russia cannot make him comfortable, pay for nurses and helpers, dress him, feed him, and find him work. Unlike England, beggars are forced onto the streets because of their infirmity, age, helplessness and not because of their addiction or illness. I would never give to anyone on the streets in England because I knew it would more than likely go towards their next bottle of gin or fix, but in Moscow money goes for food and clothing and shelter. If you are homeless in Moscow you are homeless – there is no such thing as housing for the homeless, charity soup kitchens, state support. You fight and fend for yourself the best way you can, or die. It is as simple as that. As I watched him disappear I wondered why I couldn't have done more. What had stopped me opening my wallet and giving him more? My own selfishness and self interest? My own greed? Was I really that selfish that even one pound was too much?

Changing trains at Chistye Prudy is chaotic as it is a junction between three main lines and at that time of the evening everyone was going home. Like the minibuses, everyone surges onto the carriage, giving little space for passengers to get off. There is no polite waiting to one side, you have to battle your way off the carriage through the hoards aiming to squeeze themselves on. Politeness and manners are very low on the Russian list of social priorities, even less so out on the streets, in the Metros and on the buses. Because the Metros are so cheap and so reliable, millions and millions of people use them each and every day. Apart from the main Metro stations at the major tourist sites, most of the signs are written in Cyrillic, the Russian alphabet, and therefore an extremely daunting and confusing place for most foreigners. There are no Metro maps on the actual platforms themselves, so you have to make sure you know where you are going and what line to take in advance and before you buy your tickets. Big signs in the centre of the Metro station display the list of stations on that particular line, as well as on the tunnel walls facing each platform, but you have to know where you are going and know the destination's name in Cyrillic. What is even more confusing is that connecting stations have different names and there are even a couple of stations with the same names. For example the British Embassy is on Metro Smolenskaya, but there are two Smolenskayas, both near each other but one on the blue line and the other on the purple line. Depending upon which one you get off results in either a two minute walk down a side street to the Embassy or a ten minute walk and suicidal dash across a busy six lane highway. But once you get used to it, the Metro is a quick, efficient and an extremely cheap way of travelling throughout central Moscow. Bar a rare emergency or an occasional breakdown, you can generally plan your time from arrival to destination within a few minutes. Trains run like clockwork, as soon as one train pulls away, another quickly follows. Platforms are huge and spacious and most beautifully and ornately decorated denoting a historical scene or symbolising a remarkable event or famous person. The escalators carrying the millions of passengers into the depths and bowels of the earth are some of the biggest and longest in the world. At the bottom of every escalator, in a little glass box sits a grumpy looking guard whose duty it is to look after their escalator. Normally elderly women, they sit in their little glass box day in day out watching the millions of people descend *their* escalator. If you misbehave, or sit down, or place your bag on the moving hand rail, they shout at you loudly over the loudspeaker, instructing you to stop doing whatever it was that you were doing and behave correctly. Like bloodhounds armed police mill around in small groups targeting anyone looking remotely like a foreigner – checking papers, passports and documents and eliciting illegal fines. A policeman's normal wage is equivalent to around fifty pounds a month which is not enough to survive, even in Moscow, so the majority of their salary is made up from stopping people, checking their papers, finding something wrong – even if invariably there isn't – and taking them to some dark and quiet place where they would demand money. No one wants to be locked up in a Russian prison so almost everyone pays, regardless of whether their papers are correct or not. I had the misfortune of being stopped once, and was forced to pay a ten dollar fine. At first they demanded a hundred dollars, but after a little negotiation and bartering I managed to get them down to ten. Police target foreigners because they know they have fewer rights and generally a lot more money than Russians – although during the summer they are instructed not to – it wouldn't look good targeting tourists. But if you are a foreigner at any other time of the year, or away from the centre of the city, it is almost guaranteed that you will be stopped, have your papers checked and quite possibly fined.

At Chistye Prudy station I took the short walk to Turgenevskaya for the orange line to Alekseevskaya. The Metro was packed and a sea of people flowed from one platform to another and from one train to another. I joined the flow of bodies along the connection tunnel to Turgenevskaya station. From there I would only have four stops to Alekseevskaya and my hot bowl of Borsch soup. I couldn't wait. I hated this time of the day and all these people. After just a few short minutes you feel dirty and tired and long for the fresh air and open space, even though the fresh air was minus twenty three and the open space was the centre of Moscow but anywhere, even the cold, was better than the crowded, hot, stuffy, dirty Metro.

I got off at Alekseevskaya and again followed the flow of people onto the escalator and up into the world above. The escalator led up to a small open area with kiosks selling flowers, magazines, medicines and cigarettes. In between the two rows of kiosks were the thick heavy swinging doors that led outside. With every swish of the door an intense blast of cold penetrated the Metro. People pulled down their hats, tightened their scarves and pulled up their collars as they left the warmth of the Metro for the cold of Moscow's streets. As I walked passed the kiosks towards the swinging doors something against the wall near the door caught my eye. I looked down to see a pretty dark haired girl on a small wooden platform, arms outstretched, bare hands cupped. She could have been no more than early twenties and I could immediately see she had no legs and her torso was strapped to a small wooden wheeled platform with a thick belt. Lying next to her on the wet dirty floor was a wooden block with a handle. I was steered through the doors and out of the Metro with the crowd, but I kept glancing back at this pretty girl staring up at everyone as they rushed blindly passed her, barely looking down.

"I want you to do something for me." I almost screamed to Inna as she approached me at the restaurant. I had found a seat but waited impatiently with my coat still tightly buttoned, scarf tightly wrapped and hat still firmly placed on my sweaty head and anxiously counting each second until Inna arrived.

"What's wrong?" she nervously said as I jumped up and led her back outside before she could even unbutton her coat

"Quick, I saw a girl begging at the Metro and I want to talk to her, she might have an interesting story." While I was waiting for Inna I had an idea that I could write an editorial about this girl and sell it to an English magazine. I thought that life begging on the streets of Moscow would make a fascinating human interest story and I had a notion that I could then help her in the only way I knew how – give her the money from the sale of the story.

We rushed out of the restaurant and back towards the Metro, leading Inna by the hand I was almost running through the slippery snow. Moscow Metros have separate entrances and exits and it was almost impossible to fight through the hoards of people flowing from the exit but we struggled and ignored the abuse of the passengers telling us that this was not the entrance. We eventually gave up and waited a few minutes until there was a slight lull between trains and then rushed headfirst in. I looked down to where the girl was sitting just a short while earlier, she was not there. I frantically looked around – she was nowhere to be seen.

About two months later, as I worked on my computer at home, Inna called me from her mobile.

"I have just seen her!" she cried.

I had braved the winter and the snow many times over the previous two months meeting Inna from work and hoping and praying that I would see the girl again. As the weeks passed I had virtually given up. The Russian winter was more or less ending, the snow had almost all but disappeared and, although it was now raining a great deal and still quite cold, getting around wasn't as difficult as it had been a couple of months previously. Although I still hated the minibuses and travelling into town, it became easier and easier and after a long day sitting squared eyed in front of the computer screen I would often want to travel an hour to Alekseevskaya, meet Inna and journey back home together.

"Where is she?" I shouted?

"At the Metro – shall I talk to her?"

"Yes, try and ask if we can meet her and talk to her and take some photos. Tell her I am an English journalist and that we shall write a story for an English magazine and give her some money." We had spoken about this many times and Inna knew exactly what to say.

"All right, I will see what I can do and ring you back in a minute." The line went dead. I sat by the side of the bed looking down at the phone, willing it to ring. I was so hoping that everything would be okay, that she would be happy for us to talk to her, that we could arrange to meet and that she did indeed had an interesting story to tell. As I had wondered about the life of the disabled man on the Metro, I had frequently wondered about the life of this pretty young girl.

The phone rang and I snatched at it "Hello."

"I am with her now. Her name is Maria, how about tomorrow at five pm at the Metro, is that all right?"

"Great, tell her we will see her there then. Do you have any money on you? Can you give her some now?" I wanted to make sure she would turn up.

"I have a little – I will give her a hundred roubles and we can give more tomorrow if she turns up."

"Great, see you later."

I put the phone down and breathed a huge sigh of relief. For some reason I wanted this interview more than any other I had done. After seeing that poor man with no arms begging on the Metro I felt wanted to help a little. I had seen and generally ignored poverty and hardship many times on my travels around the world but I still felt saddened and upset that people were leading this awful, miserable life. I knew nothing about this girl, apart from a pretty face looking up at me one horrible winter's day a few months ago, but hopefully I could write a good story and sell it to a magazine for a decent amount of money and help her a little – whoever she is and whatever kind of life she is leading.

The rest of the afternoon I spent preoccupied with thoughts of Maria and what we were going to talk about. I thought about what I was going to ask her – what was she doing there, where did she live, where were her family, what had happened to her, how did she lose her legs, did she have a boyfriend, what was life like for her on the streets, what were the biggest problems? So many questions, and some of them so personal. Could I actually ask them and would she actually tell me?

The next day Inna and I travelled together to meet Maria. As we exited the Metro we saw her sitting on her little wooden platform talking to a haggard, scruffy looking man selling newspapers. She turned to us, smiled, said something to the man and, with the help of her small wooden block, wheeled herself towards where we were standing. I looked down at her pretty eyes and sweet smile, greeted her in my basic Russian and shook her hand. She said something to Inna. "Shall we go and sit somewhere?" Inna asked.

"Sure, where?" I answered looking around.

We followed Maria as she wheeled herself towards a small open space, bordered by a grass verge where there were a few benches. The sun was shining, but I could see dark heavy clouds slowly building on the horizon and I hoped that we could finish before it rained. Before we started I asked Maria if I could take a photo, she agreed. I looked down my lens to this pretty little girl strapped to her wooden platform looking up at me smiling. Inna and I sat on the bench looking at Maria as she began her story.

PART TWO

Maria's Story

Based upon a true story

CHAPTER 11

Mum's Story

Based upon a true story

Chapter 1

The Journey

Spring was in the air and the snow was just beginning to melt. It was still chilly, but the weather was slowly changing. The winter had been long and hard, there had been little opportunity to go outside, apart from to school and back, and the very occasional trips to the shops with her mother, so Maria was excited.

"Do your buttons up," Maria's mother said, balancing on the corner of bed in front of her, fussing with her collar and scarf while Maria fumbled with her buttons. "Come on" her mother said, taking charge of the buttons, "Grandma's waiting and we have to catch the train. We mustn't be late now, must we?"

"Will Grandma be waiting for us at the train station?" Maria asked eagerly. She hadn't seen her grandmother all winter and was really looking forward to seeing her again. She loved her grandmother dearly.

"Of course."

"I can't wait," said Maria jumping on the spot, spinning round, giggling.

"You look so pretty today, Grandma will be proud." Maria's mother said easing herself upright of the bed. Maria did indeed look pretty in her new bright red jacket, red hat, scarf and red buckled shoes, all bought especially for this first trip to her Grandmothers since winter set in.

Maria's mother had worked hard and saved hard so that Maria could look her best.

"When will my sister be here?" Maria said, looking at her mother's swollen tummy, "I really do want someone to play with."

"Soon sweetheart, soon." Maria's mother laughed and gently stroked her tummy. "Are you sure it will be a baby girl?"

"Oh yes Mummy, of course, because I want a sister to play with so it has got to be a baby girl."

"Of course it has," Maria's mother replied, smiling. "Now put on your shoes," she said as she made a cursory check around the apartment. "And don't forget Grandma's present," she called from the kitchen.

"Got it," Maria called back, tapping the small neatly wrapped box lying on the stool next to the bed as she bent to buckle her shoes. She stood up, smoothed down her smart red jacket and tucked the small box securely under her arm. "Vecherny Zvon" truffles with hazelnut were Grandma's favorite chocolates and she would give them to her the minute she saw her waiting at the station. She couldn't wait to see grandma's face as she opened the box, her lovely smile and the kind look of anticipation in her eyes. Grandma had such lovely kind warm eyes. And of course she couldn't wait until Grandma gave her one, or two, or maybe three chocolates too! They would both giggle and hold hands and eat chocolates together.

Maria's mum pushed Maria's hat firmly on her little head and pulled Maria's gloves tightly round each finger on her little hands. They laughed as they tried to get Maria's little finger in the correct opening and not in together with her third finger.

Maria and her mother lived alone in a small apartment on the fourth floor of a typical Russian style apartment block in a small village in Western Siberia. They had moved there shortly after Maria was born. The government allocated them the apartment after her father got a job at an engineering factory nearby. He liked to drink, especially at weekends and what tiny amount he earned would almost always be spent on vodka. Maria would often hide under the sheets and cover her ears when he came home drunk. She would hear him stumbling and falling in the corridor outside, swearing that he couldn't find his key, cursing his job, his wages, his life, his wife – shouting and swearing and occasionally striking her mother. She would try to keep him quiet and not cry when he slapped her or pushed her into the corner or onto the floor and she would try to cover up the bruises with makeup the next day hoping and preying that Maria wouldn't notice. But although Maria was just five years old she did notice. She knew and understood everything.

He left them one evening almost eight months previously after a drunken, violent argument a few weeks after Maria's mother had fallen pregnant with their second child. They had not heard one word from him since, and neither did they want to. Although it was a struggle on the few roubles a month she earned stocking shelves and serving at the local supermarket, they were happier now than they ever had been. Maria never asked after her father, not once, and her mother didn't care.

"Hurry up Mummy," Maria called as she raced ahead of her mother, down the path leading away from their apartment block towards the town square and general direction of the railway station. "Mummy, hurry, hurry. Grandma's waiting." She jumped around playfully, tightly holding the pretty box containing Grandma's chocolates, kicking the remaining snow and stamping in the muddy puddles.

"Coming, don't run off, wait for me and don't get your shoes dirty!" her mother called, walking as quickly as she could. The town wasn't big and the station wasn't far, but for a woman almost eight months pregnant it was nevertheless a difficult and long walk. The paths were still quite slippery and Maria's mother had to keep calling for the excited and impatient Maria to slow down.

"Hello little Maria," an elderly lady said, stopping to look down at Maria playing in the small puddle and then up across at Maria's mother who she could see was following behind. "Where are you off to, all excited, this morning?" She asked.

"I am going to see my Grandma," she replied "and I have some chocolates for her," she said proudly showing the old lady the prettily wrapped box.

"What a lucky girl you are, and what a lucky grandmother she is," she said laughing, patting Maria on the head and stalling for time while Maria's mother slowly caught up.

"And we are going on the train!" exclaimed Maria.

"How wonderful and how exciting! Have you been on a train before?" the old lady asked.

"No," she said, a little confused. She wasn't sure whether she had or hadn't been on a train before, but she was very excited about it nevertheless.

"Well, you must remember to wave to everyone standing on the platform," she said "and they will all wave back! Hello dear," she said to Maria's mother as she finally caught up.

"Hello Mrs. Effimova, how are you today?"

"Fine dear, thank you," she said and looked down at Maria again, "Well little Maria, have a nice time at your grandmother's and mind you don't eat too many of those yummy chocolates," she said laughingly as she walked off towards the apartment block.

Maria held her mother's hand as they walked the remaining distance to the station. It didn't take them long.

Once they arrived they queued together, still holding hands and bought one adult and one child return ticket from a lady peering through a small hole in the wall that was the ticket office. She looked up at the notice board confirming the arrival time of the train they had planned to catch. Luckily they had just a few minutes to spare. Although her grandmother lived in Tumen, the biggest city in that part of Western Siberia and only about an hours journey from their town, trains didn't run that often and the next train wasn't until much later in the afternoon.

There were already quite a few people waiting on the platform. Maria's mother looked around. She needed to go to the toilet, but there were just too many people on the platform and she didn't really want to leave Maria standing there on her own. Plus the train was due any minute now. She would just have to wait until they got on the train.

Maria looked around fascinated. "Is everyone going to see their grandma too, mummy?" asked Maria, tugging on her mother's sleeve. But nobody else seemed to be holding a box of chocolates like Maria was, so she knew *her* grandmother must be the best grandmother in the world.

"No, not everyone, but some are," her mother replied looking around again and wondered if indeed she could leave Maria for a few short minutes and pop to the toilet, or perhaps Maria could come with her and wait outside.

"Why don't they have presents?" she asked

"Well, maybe because your granny is the best and deserves chocolates the most," she said looking down at Maria again. Maria knew she *did* have the best Grandma in the world and held the little box even more tightly.

They heard the whistle of the train.

"Mummy, the train is coming," Maria shouted, "I heard it mummy, it is coming." She jumped up and down excitedly, one hand holding her mothers' and the other hand tightly holding her grandmother's present. "I can see it, I can see it," she shouted looking down the tracks at a big monster coming nearer and nearer. She could see a window at the front of this strange shape, and through the window she could see two funny looking men in funny hats, looking very grumpy. "It's coming, it's coming," she shouted. People around looked down at her and smiled.

The train slowly pulled into the station, moving past her like a huge noisy smelly green beast. Maria looked up in awe at the big metal boxes and through the windows into the stained ceilings of the compartments.

"Are we going in there?" She asked.

"As soon as it stops," her mother replied.

The train shuddered to a halt and the platform became a mass of people scrambling in all directions – jostling to get on and to get off, saying "goodbyes" and "hellos." Platform traders sprang from no-where offering candy and cakes, magazines, puzzles, maps and drinks.

Maria and her mother scrambled through the broken half opened doors and onto the train. They found a seat a few compartments down from the front of the carriage.

"Now sit still," Maria's mother said.

Maria stared out of the window. So many people – like ants in the garden where she lived, scurrying back and forth. She smiled as she watched everyone on the platform, some were waving, others hugging, last farewells, emotional meetings. She could see men dressed in dirty overalls, like her father used to wear, probably on their way to work, children being lifted off the floor and hugged and kissed, old ladies with makeshift trolleys piled high with boxes and bags, and an old man on crutches standing silently with his hand held out. She stared at the man. Something was strange about him and then she saw that one of his trouser legs was hanging loose and fluttering slightly in the wind.

She turned to her mother "Look Mummy," she said pointing at the old man but just at that moment the whistle blew and the train shuddered and started to move.

"We are going Mummy," Maria said excitedly forgetting about the man. "We are going to see Grandma, hurry train, hurry!"

"Now wait here, I must use the toilet. Promise me you won't move. Okay? I won't be a minute."

"All right Mummy," replied Maria, staring out of the window enthralled with the motion of the train and with watching everyone passing by outside.

Maria's mother looked across to the bench opposite to where a fat lady in some sort of a grey uniform sat with her head bowed. "Keep and eye on her for a couple of minutes for me, will you?" she called.

The lady looked up at Maria, then at her mother and nodded.

As the train started to move and everyone started to wave, Maria stood up to get a better view. She remembered what the old lady outside their apartment had said and waved back. She wondered if they were all waving at her. They must be, she thought. The fat lady opposite looked up briefly and saw Maria standing at the window waving. She grunted, closed her eyes and let her head fall forward again. She was tired, a little drunk and just wanted to sleep.

Maria carefully placed her grandmother's box on the seat and rushed the short distance down the aisle to the carriage door to get a better look at everyone before the train completely left the platform. The carriage door had not closed properly and little Maria could see everyone quite clearly between the jammed doors. She held the inside handle to one of the doors and leaned out slightly to wave at all the people waving back at her. She thought she heard someone shout "Go back inside little girl," but she couldn't be sure and leaned out even more. She loved the feel of the cool air rushing against her face as the train slowly picked up speed. She watched fascinated and the people grew smaller and smaller and the train got faster and faster. A couple of minutes into the journey the train jolted as it suddenly switched tracks and Maria's right foot slipped and dangled in mid air, bouncing against the side of the train. She desperately clung to the metal railing as the wind pulled and tugged at her little body. "Mummy!" she screamed. No one heard her as the wind through the open doors became louder and louder as the train picked up speed, and no one in the carriage saw her as she was hidden behind the solid metal carriage divider. Her other leg slid off and her hands slithered down the icy cold rail. "Mummy!" she screamed again. Maria's feet bounced and banged against the side of the train as she desperately tried to keep hold of the rail but her little hands couldn't hold on any longer. Maria felt herself slowly slip and heard a horrible crunch of her tiny bones and a terrible tearing and ripping just below her waist. She fell onto the hard frozen earth below and rolled, over and over again, banging and smashing herself on the hard metal tracks.

She didn't know how long she had been laying there. She opened her eyes and looked up at the wonderful clear blue sky. She stared at the beautiful fluffy white clouds rushing past and watched as a bird whizzed backwards and forwards, up and down. At first there was no sound, just silence and stillness. She sensed a light breeze on her face and in her eyes. Then she heard a kind of rumbling sound, which seemed to get louder and louder. She looked up and saw a huge dark blurred shape coming towards her. At first she wasn't quite sure what it was, and then remembered where she was going and that this huge shape was a train and it seemed to be coming directly at her. She wanted to stand up and run, but she couldn't move. "I am here!" she screamed, "I am here!" but the train kept coming. She raised one hand in the air and waved and waved as hard as she could.

"Is that a red light?" asked one driver to the other.

"Can't be, there are no signals on this stretch of track," the other replied.

"It must be – look," said the other as he strained forward, squinting his eyes to see the small speck of red that seemed to lay illuminated in the centre of the track ahead.

"Just a piece of red cloth," the other replied.

Feeling something was not quite right, the driver eased off the controls and started to slow a little. They weren't far from the station and few seconds delay wasn't going to make much difference.

Nodding to himself "It is a piece of cloth," he confirmed, but just as he was about to accelerate, the piece of cloth moved.

"Oh my God!!!" The driver shouted slamming on the brakes. The train shuddered to a stop. The driver locked the breaks, jumped out of the carriage onto the ground below and raced along the tracks. The second driver followed.

"Oh my God, Oh my God," the driver cried as he approached little Maria lying helpless between the tracks, tears flowing down his cheeks.

Little Maria looked up at the two grimy faces with funny hats looking down at her. She wondered why one of them was crying. Soon other blurred faces started to appear around her, crying and sobbing, looking down at her and saying "Poor little thing." Mother's ushered their inquisitive children away, grandmothers gasped and wailed.

She felt someone gently pick her up and ask her name.

"Maria," she said, "I am going to see my Grandmother." She looked around at everyone huddling around her and smiled. She didn't like it when people cried. Maria closed her eyes and fell unconscious.

"Maria," called her mother as she entered the carriage and noticed the neatly wrapped present in the spot Maria was sitting in just a few minutes earlier. "Maria!" she shouted louder. She looked outside and saw the trees rushing by and down again at the box of chocolates. "Where's my daughter? I asked you to keep a look out for her," she yelled at the fat lady in uniform sitting hunched up.

"I think she went for a walk," she looked up and said groggily, pointing to the next carriage.

Maria's mother frantically opened the door leading into passageway between carriages and felt the cold and wind hit her. She saw the door to the carriage was broken and slightly ajar. "No, no no no," she said over and over again as she rushed into the next carriage.

"Has a little girl come past here?" she hysterically asked passenger after passenger making her way down the carriage. Everyone said no, they had not seen a little girl. She rushed to the next carriage, and yelled, "Has anyone seen my little girl?" Curious passengers looked round the compartment walls shaking their heads – no one had seen a little girl. An elderly man got up from his seat and said he would go further down the train and ask and that she should go back to her seat, just in case she was hiding somewhere.

"Thank you, thank you." She sobbed. "She is five years old and is wearing a little red jacket and red hat with a bobble in the middle. Please find her," she pleaded.

Maria's mother rushed sobbing through the carriage back towards where they had been sitting. As she passed the passageway where the carriage doors were broken and wedged ajar she glanced down at the floor and noticed Maria's small red glove sitting in the corner.

Maria woke up and looked around her. She stared up at the white ceiling and across at the white walls and then at the people in white coats standing around her. Her eyes hurt with the bright lights shining down at her. She was so frightened and tried to remember what happened. She couldn't remember anything and tears started to roll down her cheeks. She wanted her mummy. "Where's my mummy?" she sobbed. She wanted to tell her mummy that it wasn't her fault, she just wanted to wave to everyone. She didn't do anything wrong, promise mummy. She tried to speak again but no words came out.

"Sshh little Maria, now go to sleep." She heard a soft voice whisper gently in her ear and felt a hand with a cloth go over her nose and mouth. The cloth smelt funny, but she soon fell into a deep sleep.

When Maria opened her eyes again she saw a beautiful blue sky and a big fluffy white cloud. But this time the cloud wasn't moving, and floated just about her. She stared up at the cloud, wondering why it seemed to be getting closer and closer. The cloud looked so lovely, so pretty, so calm. She felt that the cloud was a good cloud, that it was guarding her, looking after her, keeping her safe. She felt as if it was her friend. It seemed that she knew the cloud and the cloud knew her. She smiled up at the cloud and the cloud seemed to smile back. Through her blurred tired eyes the cloud slowly turned into her mummy's face.

"Mummy!" she tried to shout, "Mummy!" She was so glad her mummy had found her, that now everything would be all right. She was frightened that she was going to be told off for misbehaving, for not sitting still and in one place. She didn't want to be told off, she just wanted to go home. Tears rolled down her cheeks. She looked up and saw tears running down her mummy's cheeks – her mummy was crying too.

"Don't cry mummy," she whispered. "Everything is all right now. You have found me now and I promise I won't be naughty again. I promise Mummy. Can we go to Grandma's now, please?" She looked around for her grandmother's little box of chocolates she had so carefully guarded. "Where's grandma's chocolates?" she asked.

"Oh my little Maria," cried her mother, trying to wipe away the endless stream of tears from her eyes. She bent over and hugged Maria, kissing her, splashing her face with her tears. "Please don't cry Mummy," Maria said, "We can get Grandma some more chocolates."

"Oh my little Maria," her mother replied, wiping Maria's cheeks.

"I need a wee wee mummy." Maria said raising herself a little. She felt strange, a little odd.

"Wait – I will help you and get you a bedpan," her mother replied bending down to get the pan from under the bed.

"Don't be silly Mummy, I can do it myself," Maria said pushing herself upright as much as she could. Before her mummy could stop her, Maria took hold of the blanket and threw it to one side, preparing to climb out of the bed. She couldn't move. Maria looked down to where her legs should have been and saw two small bandaged stumps of white cloth. Her face contorted with pain and confusion. "Mummy" she screamed, "Where are my legs?"

Suddenly pain ripped through her body tearing her apart. She screamed as she remembered falling off the carriage, and seeing her legs go under the huge wheels of the train. She screamed as she felt the bones splinter and break and felt her legs tear away from her body. There was so much unbearable pain, ripping through her tiny body and piercing her mind. Maria's mind and body could not bear more physical pain. She fell unconscious.

Chapter 2

Just Sleeping

Everyone lost hope of ever seeing Maria alive again. The horrific injuries and the intense psychological trauma were more than most adults could bare, let alone a small five year old child. Everybody thought that Maria would never wake up. For two years she laid unconscious, alone, while her grandmother looked after her. Her grandmother knew that Maria was only sleeping and believed without doubt or hesitation that everything would eventually be all right, that she would one day wake up and they would go all home together. Many times her mother, in despair, would plead with the doctors to turn off the machines that were keeping her daughter alive and to disconnect the apparatus that surrounded her poor invalid child. She didn't want Maria to suffer any longer, she wanted Maria to go to a safe, happy place full of little children and fairies and a beautiful blue sky with fluffy white clouds. She wanted Maria to be happy and not to feel any sadness or despair or pain. She recognised that, even if Maria did survive and did eventually wake up, from now on her life would not be easy.

At night her mother would dream about little Maria running in the snow and jumping up and down in the puddles on that fateful day they left their apartment to catch the train. She would see Maria climbing the big old tree outside their apartment, running in the summer school race, skipping in the park, climbing the wooden play frames, running with their neighbour's dog, being chased and chasing other children. Every morning she would wake up crying into her pillow, missing Maria so much it was virtually unbearable. She prayed Maria would get better yet she somehow also prayed that she would quietly and painlessly pass away into the other world. She couldn't imagine a world for her daughter without legs, a world confined to a wheelchair, having to be pushed around and missing out on everything a young child should experience. They were, of course, other disabled children living in their village, but very few and they were rarely seen – they hardly ever went outside and spent most of their lives hidden away, unseen, cooped up in front of the television in their tiny rundown apartments. Getting around for someone with such disabilities in a small Siberian town was virtually impossible – paths were terrible, steps impractical, access to most places impossible. The thought of Maria sitting in her chair while others played and danced and ran around made her mother's sorrow greater and cry harder. She blamed herself for what happened to her gorgeous little daughter, if she hadn't have gone to the toilet, if she hadn't have left Maria in that carriage alone, if she hadn't chosen a carriage with a broken door, if she hadn't have trusted her daughter's welfare to a drunken fat woman, Maria would be with her now talking about everything and anything, laughing and giggling and being silly. Instead, her beautiful little daughter was lying unconscious in a hospital bed while she cried night after night wishing that things could all change, that time could be turned back.

Maria wasn't in pain, she was just sleeping and dreaming of all the beautiful things in the world. She dreamt of the first day of summer when she and her mum went down to the lake. It was a lovely sunny day and the lake glistened like stars in the sky. Maria excitedly took her shoes and socks off, hitched up her skirt and ran to the water line. Even though it was summer the water was still very cold and Maria gave a quick shriek as she touched the water with her big toe.

"Ouch, it is so cold Mummy," Maria shouted while looking down at the water hoping it would suddenly turn a little warmer. It didn't. Maria slowly and nervously eased her whole foot in, inch by inch, shrieking loudly as the cold numbed her tiny feet.

"Are you going to paddle or not?" Maria's mother called to her, laughingly, as she followed Maria to the water line and watched as she tried to immerse her foot. "Go on, in you go," she said, giving her a gentle push on the shoulder.

"Mummy, don't," cried Maria, "it is so cold." Then suddenly both feet were in and she was splashing around as though the cold had vanished and the water was as warm as her bath. "Come on then," Maria called back to her mother. Maria's mother crouched down and took off her two shoes and eased herself slowly into the water.

Maria dreamt of the two of them, paddling and splashing around in the water, trying not to get their clothes wet, shrieking with the cold, yet laughing and giggling and having so much fun together. She saw other children running up and down the sandy shore, shouting to one another, playing Pioneer ball, playing "catch me," throwing Frisbees and playing hopscotch. She could see other children skipping and eating ice cream and families sitting together having picnics – the lake was such a fun place in the summer.

Suddenly the lake turned into ice. It was winter and Maria was kneeling tying up the laces to her skating shoes. She looked up and saw all the people in their woollen hats and tightly wrapped scarves skating round and round an imaginary shape in the centre of the small lake. Maria loved to skate and almost every weekend when it wasn't snowing, she and her mother would go down to the lake and skate together, until Maria found some friends, which invariably didn't take long. Maria's mother would then stand on the side of the lake smiling as she watched Maria and her friends play. Maria waved as she whizzed passed her mother, laughing with her little friend Sofia who was chasing her. "Can't catch me, can't catch me," Maria called to Sofia.

"Yes I can, Yes I can," Sofia shouted back. They weren't going very fast but Maria thought that they were as fast as lightening. In her dreams Maria looked down at herself and her friend playing together on the icy lake and watched as they both circled the lake, calling to one another and playing and laughing. It started to snow, ever so lightly, and Maria could feel the small flakes get into her eyes as she sped her way around the lake. In her coma Maria's eyes fluttered a little as she dreamed of the icy lake and little Sofia just a few feet behind her, giggling as she tried to grab Maria's coat-tail.

The lake turned into the playing field next to the kindergarten. It was the sports day, the day before the summer holidays, and all the children were smartly dressed in their white t-shirts and red shorts. Maria sat with all her friends on the grass alongside the track, with parents, brothers and sisters, grandmothers and grandfather sitting behind on blankets and jackets. Maria kept peering back, occasionally giving a little smile and wave to her mother, who smiled and waved back. Maria was going to run in the next race. She thought about the pretty certificate she would get for winning and remembered the plaque in the foyer of the kindergarten above the entrance thanking their "Mother Country" for their happy childhood.

"All children in the sack race put your hands up," said

Maria's teacher, towering over all the little children, huddled, giggling, excited.

Maria reached for the sky. She was going to run like the wind and make her mummy really proud and happy.

"Everyone over there at the start line," her teacher called, pointing to a white piece of ribbon anchored down with two clothes pegs. Two teachers ushered the children together as they scrambled up and over to the start line.

"Come on everyone, line up," said the teacher. Maria and all her friends lined up, each with one foot just touching the little white ribbon trailing along the grassy floor. The teacher grabbed the bundle of sacks lying in a pile and placed one sack in front of each of the children lining up ready to run.

"When I say go, everyone get into your sack and bounce and bounce as fast as you can down the track,." called out the teacher, "you can all bounce, can't you?" she cried.

"Yes," cried everyone.

"I can't hear you – you can all bounce can't you?" the teacher called putting her hand to her ear.

"Yes," cried the children even louder.

"Those that bounce the best will get a sweet." Maria loved sweets and would bounce and bounce and bounce until she couldn't bounce any more.

"Ready, Steady, Go!" her teacher shouted and all the little children raced forward, as fast as they could, scrambling into their sack and bouncing their way down the short track. From the corner of her eye Maria could see her mother jumping up and down, cheering and shouting and calling her name. She could see her friend Sofia's mother doing the same, in fact she could see all the parents and relatives and friends of all the children jumping and screaming and shouting and waving their flags. Maria jumped her way down the track to the end and to a huge cheer.

"Everyone jumped so well," the teacher called "everyone

can have a sweet." The children cheered as they struggled out of their sacks, dumping them where they fell, and huddled round the teacher with their hands out stretched waiting for a tasty sweet.

Shortly after the accident Maria was moved from the small poorly equipped clinic in her village to the region's biggest hospital in Tumen, the town her grandmother lived. For two years Maria laid unconscious in the hospital bed sleeping and dreaming about all the wonderful fun things. Every single day Maria's grandmother would visit her, carefully cleaning her wounds and changing her bandages, gasping tearfully each and every time she saw those two raw stumps on her granddaughter's beautiful tiny body. No one touched little Maria apart from her. She would delicately clean the healing wounds and carefully cover them again with fresh linen she personally brought to the hospital. She didn't trust the hospital or the products and she would spend most of her meagre pension buying new liniments and ointments, bandages and dressing. She would wash Maria every single day, change her clothes, clean her teeth, cut her nails, brush her hair, read to her, talk to her or just sit by her side holding her delicate, little hand. There were many days when her grandmother went without food so that her granddaughter could have fresh dressing and clean clothes.

Maria's wounds were slowly healing, but her grandmother knew the scars in her mind would remain with her forever. Time passed, day after day, week after week, month after month. Soon a year had passed but every single day without fail, through rain, snow and low temperatures, Maria's grandmother would get up at about seven am, carefully organize the things she had to take for that day, pack everything tightly in a small bag, wrap herself up against the bleak Siberian winter and walk to the hospital.

Lots of people in the town knew about Maria and her grandmother. Sometimes the neighbours would bring a little something to help – some warm food, an extra blanket or a flower for Maria's bed. The old ladies sitting on crates behind their makeshift stalls selling vegetables and cigarettes would greet her every morning with a nod or a smile and occasionally wish Maria well. She would pass the same people queuing every morning for the minibus, the same ladies cleaning the streets after the snow had melted and the same people returning home from work every afternoon. As she made her daily trundle back and forth to the hospital she looked around at everyone preoccupied with their own lives and she wondered what kind of lives they led and what a life her little Maria would lead. Unlike so many women she passed on the streets rushing back to their homes and their families at the end of the day, she knew that Maria would never be able to rush anywhere and probably never have a family and children to rush home to.

Almost two years to the day a woman was walking her dog in the forest near to the railway tracks. It was a cold day, same as it was two years ago. There was just a slight breeze and white clouds dotted the clear blue sky. The woman's dog lazily trailed behind its owner, sniffing the ground, rummaging through the foliage.

"Here Ash," the lady turned and called and Ash pricked up its ears and trundled reluctantly towards the lady, who was arranging its lead. Suddenly the dog stopped in its tracks and started at something in the distance. It barked once and rushed forward a few paces, and barked again. The lady turned and looked, but could see nothing.

"It's just a rabbit," she said, but the dog barked again and rushed further forward, past the lady, completely ignoring her calls to heel.

"What is it Ash?" the lady asked and strained to see something bright half hidden in the undergrowth. "Go and fetch it," she said and the dog raced forward. The lady followed expecting the dog to pick it up and bring it proudly back to her. But the dog stopped and stared and barked loudly at the brightly coloured object.

"What have you found?" the lady said as she approached the agitated dog. She bent down at the object, tugged at it and pulled a child's red buckled shoe out from under the layer of grass and old leaves.

"Oh my goodness!" She gasped. The lady with the dog had heard about the poor little girl that lost both legs in a terrible accident on the railway tracks a couple of years ago and she felt that this was her shoe. No one ever found Maria's legs, they were presumed eaten by the wild dogs that roamed free in the forest, or by some other animal. Although the lady didn't know the little girl personally, she knew of her mother and where she lived and, carefully wrapping the shoe in a sheet of newspaper she had wrapped some apples with, she decided to take it back to her. As they walked away from the forest towards the village the dog kept tight by her side, staring protectively up at the wrapped package as though somehow sensing sympathy and compassion.

It was early evening when the lady finally managed to finish what she had to do at home and walk to the apartment block where she knew Maria's mother lived. For the few hours she was at home, the shoe, carefully wrapped in newspaper, sat in the centre of the kitchen table, the dog sat unmoving staring fixedly at the little bundle.

"Hello," she said almost in a whisper to Maria's mother as she opened the door to her apartment. Taking it carefully from her bag, the lady fumbled with the small package, not at all knowing what to say or what to do. "I found this in the forest this morning," she said timidly, frightened. Maybe she should have left it where it was. "I think this might be your daughter's, I think you might want it back."

Maria's mother looked at the small package in the lady's hand as it was carefully offered to her.

"Won't you come in?" she asked

"No, no thank you." She turned away to leave.

"Thank you," she called as the lady disappeared through the doorway.

Maria's mother stared at the small package in front of her. She placed it gently on the kitchen table.

The next day Maria woke up from her long sleep. Two years had passed, she was now seven years old. She opened her eyes and looked around. Somehow she seemed to know where she was. She wasn't frightened, she just lay silently looking across the room and out of the window. She felt a little hungry but lay waiting for someone to enter the room. As usual her grandmother made the daily journey to the hospital. It was another nice clear day, the sun was shining. She walked past a hospital orderly mopping the floor and greeted her with her usual polite "Good Morning." That same orderly had been cleaning the floors of the hospital ever since grandmother made her first harrowing visit two years ago. No one was crying now, everything had settled into routine and quiet order. She walked down the corridor and straight into Maria's room, wishing her a good morning, not ever expecting her to reply.

"Good morning grandma, I am a little hungry."

Chapter 3

Back Home

Fearing Maria might fall back into her coma, Maria's grandmother was frightened to leave her, even for a second and even though she was hungry. She spent the next hour or so sitting on Maria's bed caressing her hand and stroking her hair and holding back her tears. It seemed suddenly as if the past two years never existed, that it was all a dream and that Maria had just had a good night's sleep. As she caressed Maria's arm she quietly told her everything that had happened over the past two years. Maria lay silently listening, enjoying the sound of her grandmother's voice and gentle touch. Her grandmother told her she had not been well and had slept for a very long time and Maria listened sleepily, not understanding what had happened or how long she had been asleep.

"And you have a new sister," her grandmother said. Maria's eyes lit up and a huge smile covered her face.

"Really?" she cried.

"Really! Her name is Nadezhda." Maria's mother had named the baby Nadezhda, the Russian word for "hope."

The orderly cleaning outside heard the little girl's voice and burst into the room. "She's awake!" she hollered and ran back out and down the corridor towards the nurse's station shouting "She's awake, little Maria's awake." A few minutes later the bed was surrounded by almost every member of the ward's staff.

It seemed that Maria somehow understood what had happened to her and was not at all troubled with the loss of her legs. She had had many dreams where she saw herself sitting in a chair not being able to get out, or having to be carried, or being unable, in some strange way, not to be able to do the things that others were doing in her dreams. They were never nightmares – she knew and understood that the girl she was seeing in her dreams was herself, she had her face and her eyes and she was always smiling back at Maria, telling her not to worry and that it was going to be fine. It seemed in some strange, extraordinary and unfathomable way her mind was preparing her for the time she would eventually wake up and was helping her to come to terms with what had happened.

As soon as she felt comfortable about leaving Maria for a few minutes, her grandmother telephoned Maria's mother at work. Her boss had a car and, after she frantically made arrangements with a neighbour to look after Nadezhda, he agreed to drive her to the hospital. He couldn't drive fast enough. Maria's mother spent the rest of that day and all that night at Maria's bedside, talking and laughing as they had two years ago, before the accident. The following morning she returned home to Nadezhda.

A few days later Maria moved out of the hospital that had been her home for the past two years and into the familiar and comforting home she missed so much. That morning Maria's mother had woken up early and asked a neighbour to look after Nadezhda. She then caught the train – the same train that had so horribly disabled Maria– and Maria's grandmother waited for her at the station, as she had waited for them two years ago. For Maria's mother, that journey, back then, was the longest journey of her life.

She had frantically searched up and down each and every carriage. Finally realising her daughter was no longer on the train she sat hysterical, crying, with her face buried in her hands and the box of chocolates on her lap. The guard and a few passengers had sat around her, comforting her but there was nothing they could do until they reached the next stop. Maria's grandmother, waiting for them on the platform, noticed there were a few more police than normal but thought nothing of it. After they had rushed Maria to a local emergency clinic, the other train stations on route were notified and police were sent to each station and told to keep an eye out for a report of a missing child. At that time they didn't know which stop Maria was due to get off. As soon as Maria's mother left the train, screaming and falling into her mother's arms, the police surrounded them. After her mother hysterically told them what had happened they quickly ushered them into a waiting police car and back to their village where Maria was laying at the clinic critically ill. That was two years ago and still the fear and trauma haunted them both.

Maria's grandmother brought an empty cloth bag where she would put the few possessions Maria had by her bedside. They walked together to the bus stop and waited until the bus to the hospital appeared. The day before, Maria's grandmother had arranged with the hospital for an ambulance to take Maria back home. At first the hospital refused, saying it was simply not possible to take an ambulance away from the hospital for the two to three hour journey. But after she offered a small sum of money to both the administrator and the ambulance driver, a spare ambulance was miraculously found.

Maria was still mentally just five years old and so things seemed very strange and confusing but she knew she couldn't wait to get home. She would have left the day she awoke if the doctors and nurses hadn't insisted she stay a few more nights for tests and examinations. More than anything she wanted to see her little sister, the little sister she somehow remembered she so much wanted to play with. Two years seemed just like one night and she found it quite hard to understand that in her so called "one night" of sleep her sister had been born and was now almost two years old.

"Mummy, Grandma." Maria called as they entered her room.

They all hugged and kissed and a nurse was stood by the bedside. Maria was already washed and dressed and waiting to leave. A doctor walked into the room just as Maria was being lifted from the bed onto a wheelchair that had been positioned by the side of the bed.

"So, you are finally going home, little Maria?" the doctors said, beaming. "We'll miss you, you know," he said, patting her on the head. "But you be sure to come back and visit us someday." He turned to Maria's mother "You will just have to sign a couple of discharge forms before you leave – they are at the reception desk." Maria's mother nodded and Maria's grandmother pushed Maria and her wheelchair out into the corridor. As the door closed behind them, she turned to take one last look into the room that had been so much a part of her life.

As she was wheeled down the corridor nurses and doctors and orderlies and even a couple of patients hugged her and kissed her and wished her well. She somehow felt like a beautiful princess sitting on a throne with all her subjects around her. The doors of the ambulance were already open and as she was carefully wheeled into the back, everyone shouted goodbye and waved. She waved back and the doors were closed and the ambulance moved off. She had never been in an ambulance before and sat excitedly with her grandmother and mother looking around. It didn't look much. The sliding window to the driver's compartment slid open and the man in the front asked if they were all right.

"Would you like me to put on the siren?" he asked Maria, smiling.

"Can you?" she asked.

The man bent over and flicked up a switch and the siren started. Maria giggled.

Although she didn't remember her room, it had remained almost exactly as she left it – her dolls were carefully placed on top of the bed, her dresses, now too small, regularly washed and ironed and kept with her jumpers and t-shirts, blouses and skirts in her little wardrobe opposite her bed, her socks and underwear still neatly folded. The only difference was that Maria's bedroom was now also her sister's bedroom, and a cot was now placed next to Maria's bed and her sister's clothes next to hers.

It was going to be a little cramped as it was agreed that, for a short time and until she was feeling much better, her grandmother would stay at home with them. Maria's mother was working almost full-time, as well as trying to look after Maria's two year old sister and having her grandmother living there would help the family immeasurably. Maria had become so much a daily part of her grandmother's life that she could not think of what a day would be like without having little Maria to look after. There was nothing else in her life and she could not remember what life was like before her daily visits to the hospital. Maria's grandmother was happy that she helping her family – she knew it would have been impossible for Maria's mother to work full-time as well as look after Maria and her baby sister.

Maria's mother hadn't managed to get to the hospital as much as she wanted, although she always spent her days off sitting by the hospital bed reading and chatting and singing lullabies, but then only when she managed to find a friend to look after Nadezhda. The trains ran infrequently and Maria's mother didn't know anyone with a car. She never brought Nadezhda to visit Maria in hospital – the fear of taking her on to a train was just too great. She could hardly cope herself, every minute of every journey she took she sat shaking and tearful, but now that Maria's grandmother was staying she could spend a little more time with Maria. Grandma would help with the cooking and cleaning and washing the clothes and doing the shopping while Maria's mother spent time with her daughters – they had so much fun together before the accident.

At first everyone was kind and helpful and felt sorry for little Maria. She had many visitors and helpers and was given lots of gifts. People would bring round a few chocolates or biscuits or freshly made jam, or even a little toy. People she didn't even know would stop them in the street, look down at Maria sitting in her chair, with her pretty dresses and ribbons in her hair and a blanket thrown over her lap to hide the space where her legs should have been and say how awful it all was. They would wish her their best and if there is anything they could do to help. Maria would peer up and nod as they patted her on the head or stroked her hair and then went on their way. Almost everyone in the village had heard about Maria – the little girl that lost her legs in a train accident. For the first year so many people offered their support and help.

Maria was seven years old when she left hospital and a few days after returning home she asked her mother if she could go to school. Her wounds had long ago healed, she was as bright and bubbly and as cheerful and friendly as she was before her accident and she hated the thought of having to spend most of her time cooped up in their tiny apartment. She really wanted to go to school, to see her friends again, to play with them and laugh. She had an infectious little giggle that so many people adored, and it was a long time since anyone had heard that giggle. Her mother and grandmother didn't really want her to go to school as they feared the torments and the physical difficulties she would encounter, but they realised it would not be right to keep her away from other children her own age and understood fully Maria's need to lead as full and normal life as possible, even though there would sometimes be huge difficulties.

There was also going to be a problem with her age. Because she was still mentally only five years old, it was going to be difficult putting her with a class of seven year olds. A few weeks earlier her mother had gone to see the school to discuss this dilemma in detail and it was decided that, for the time being at least, she would be placed in preparatory class along with other children roughly the same mental age. This seemed fairer and a lot easier for Maria. She had missed two years of schooling and an awful lot of learning. Even though she was physically two years bigger than the children around her, she was still a five year old.

The first day at school Maria was so excited. The night before she could hardly sleep and kept tossing and turning and wishing the night would pass quickly. She called out for her mother three or four times, asking for water or a biscuit, or just for some company, someone to cuddle and hold while she tried to nod off again. Maria's mother and grandmother tossed and turned and couldn't sleep either, but for different reasons, they were nervous and scared and wished the night would pass as slowly as possible.

Maria finally woke about six am, and could hear someone in the kitchen.

"Mummy," she called as she looked across the room to where her sister was snuggled sleeping soundly. Her sister was the only one in the house that had had good night's sleep.

Her grandmother came into the room and smiled down at Maria, who had propped herself up against the head-board.

"Are you ready for your first day at school?" she whispered quietly, not wanting to wake her sister.

"I think so," said Maria.

"Are you a little nervous?" her grandmother asked.

"I think so," Maria replied, yawning. "Where's mummy?"

"In the kitchen. Come on, let's get you washed and dressed and ready for school. Are you hungry?"

"Uh huh."

Maria's grandmother wheeled Maria's chair over to the bed while she wiggled her body to the side. She wasn't yet used to her chair, although she wanted to be as independent as possible, she still needed a helping hand getting from the bed into the chair. Maria's grandmother leaned across and hooked her arms under Maria's and, on a "one, two, three," lifted Maria into her chair.

"You are getting a heavy lump," her Grandmother said jokingly, scuffing Maria's hair.

Maria wheeled herself into the bathroom, washed her face and brushed her hair, and then into the kitchen.

"Good morning sweetheart," Maria's mother said, kissing Maria on her cheek. "Are you ready for school?" she asked.

"Grandma's just asked me that," Maria replied.

"Are you ready for breakfast then?"

"Sure am."

As Maria sat at the little wooden breakfast table, her sister called from the bedroom.

"Coming," her mother called. She disappeared into the bedroom returning holding Maria's sister.

"Do you want to come to school with me today?" Maria, with a mouth full of black bread and jam, said to her sister.

Nadezhda sister nodded, rubbing her eyes, still half asleep and not really understanding what was going on.

"Maybe another day," she replied.

Maria's mother stooped down and Maria kissed her sister on the cheek. He sister reached out and poked a finger in the bread and jam Maria was eating. Maria looked up at her sister and screwed her face in disgust. "Yuck!" she said, eyeing the bread with her sister's finger imprinted into it.

"I think you might be hungry too!" said her mother carrying her sister over to the other side of the table and plonked her on the seat.

"And you're getting heavy too!" she said playfully poking a finger in Nadezhda's tummy, which made her smile. She turned to put some milk on the stove.

"You can come to school with me one day," Maria said in between a bite full of bread.

Nadezhda looked at Maria confused.

"The day will come soon enough," her grandmother said, pouring the warm milk into Maria's cup and her sister's beaker. "Now eat up and hurry along, we don't want you to be late on your first day at school, do we?"

All eyes were on Maria and her mother as she was wheeled through the school gates. There was no ramp over the few steps up into the school building so Maria's mother turned Maria's chair about face and gently pulled her up each step, step by step with everyone standing around watching. Maria smiled and gave a shy little wave to the children gathered around. One of the children ran up to her. It was Sofia, whom she remembered from kindergarten and from her dreams, and who she used to play with long ago before her accident. Sofia hugged Maria and walked by the side of her chair as she was pushed down the short corridor towards the head teacher who had just immerged from her office.

"So this is little Maria," said the kindly looking head-mistress. "Hello Maria. Welcome to our school. I see you have found a friend already?" she said looking at Sofia. Maria nodded and smiled.

"She will be fine with us," she said looking up at Maria's mother." We have made a few provisions for her, the best we could. Don't worry yourself, she will be all right."

"Thank you," she replied and then looked down at Maria. "OK sweetheart, see you at the end of the day. Have a nice time," Maria's mother said, bending down kissing Maria on the cheek.

"Don't worry, I will look after her," little Sofia said and hugged her once more.

Maria's mother turned away and walked back down the corridor with tears streaming down her cheeks.

The hardest thing for Maria was watching all her friends play and run around and have fun while she could only sit in her little wheelchair longing to join them. She missed playing "catch me" with her friend Sofia the most. Sofia had found another friend to play "catch me" which, at first, made Maria really angry, and then a little sad. Time and time again, when she sat outside by the side of the play-ground watching everyone play, she would remember her dream of Sofia trying to grab Maria's coat on the ice rink, laughing and giggling and whizzing round and round as fast as lightening, "Catch me" used to be her favorite game and she wished those days would return that she could once again chase Sofia and Sofia could chase her. Instead she sat in her little chair while everyone around her rushed about.

Most of the children were fine and kind and occasionally helpful, but, like in every school, some taunted her and called her names. She knew she was different but was deter-mined to be strong and not to let the taunts affect her, but secretly late at night she would often cry into her pillow.

Maria's mother and grandmother would also lay awake in the living room where they both slept staring up at the ceiling listening to Maria sobbing herself to sleep. Only when there was silence would they fall asleep themselves.

Growing up without legs wasn't as hard as Maria, her family and everyone around her had thought it was going to be. They had eventually managed to get the local housing association to build a small ramp over the steps into her apartment block. The school was only a few minutes away and they too managed to get a small ramp built over the few steps into the building. She was a bright girl and quickly caught up the missing two years and within just eight short months of attending school and studying hard at home she was back amongst children of her own age.

They couldn't go anywhere as they didn't have a car and it was too difficult getting a wheelchair on and off the bus and so they were generally confined to the vicinity of where they lived. But there was a park nearby and on warm days after school Maria would be taken by either her mother or grandmother for a walk. Maria liked the park as she could watch the butterflies flutter over the grass and between the flowers and listen to the bees and stare at the birds circling above and the fluffy white clouds passing by. She watched with envy as children climbed and played on the frames and apparatus that were to be found in most parks and open areas in her village. Most of the children would rush over and say hello, spending a few minutes with Maria, chatting about the things young children chat about, and then they would be off, back onto the apparatus, swinging and sliding and playing while Maria sat and watched. She laughed as they laughed and imagined herself climbing with them as they climbed.

Although cramped their home was a happy home, with lots of fun and laughter and silliness that Maria remembered so fondly from when it was just her and her mother. Her grandmother was sometimes overbearing and occasionally bossy but there were rarely any major disagreements and hardly ever a raised voice or angry word. Mostly it was fun and they all had a good time together. Maria's grandmother was an enormous help and without her her mother simply couldn't cope. While Maria's mother was at work and Maria and her sister at school and kindergarten, Maria's grandmother washed and cleaned and cooked. She would also collect the girls from school as they invariable finished before her mother finished work. It wasn't always easy, but they fell into a routine that suited everyone. Maria was learning to live without legs. Her arms became strong and she became more and more independent, preferring to wheel than to be wheeled. She also developed an inner strength, a power not to be afraid of the world around her. She ignored the occasional taunts and cruelty of others – she grew to be confident in herself and her abilities. She loved school and when all her other classmates were going out or hanging around, she locked herself in her room and studied. She knew she could never go to the local social club, or cruise with her friends, or go to parties, or go out for walks in the forest, or go to the swimming baths, so she studied and read instead. She wasn't the top of the class, but she wasn't at the bottom either and she knew in herself that she was better at school than many of the students that had legs.

Time passed and a new man entered their life. Her mother met him at a New Years party for the employees at her work. It wasn't a big party, but employees and their partners were both invited. One of her female colleagues, who was also single, said that rather than go to the party alone she was going to bring an old school friend. He was just a friend – they had known each other since Fourth Grade at school. Tall, well-built, handsome with rough workers hands, deep dark eyes and a warm smile. It had been a long while since Maria's mother had been in the company of a man and she was secretly delighted as he appeared to attach himself to her. Although she had had little time for romance since Maria's accident and, it seemed, even less time to think about it, as Maria grew older her mother thought more and more about the possibility. She was lonely for male company and the affection and warmth that a man would give her. Maria's friend mingled with the others at the party, occasionally glancing over and grinning broadly at the two sitting away from everyone chatting together quietly in the corner.

Maria's mother started to see Nikoly more often, occasionally meeting him after work or at the weekend. They would walk, or go to the small cinema, or sit in a café – she drinking coffee and he drinking vodka. Maria's mother didn't like the fact that he drank, it reminded her of her ex-husband, but he didn't seem to drink that much and anyway, all Russian men drank. There was nothing that she could do to change the drinking habits of almost every man in Russia. Nevertheless and aside from the vodka he seemed a good man and the only man, for a very long time, that had shown her any attention and affection. It wouldn't be long before Maria and her sister would grow up and leave home, going to some university somewhere, or even go to Moscow, and her mother was getting older. She didn't want to lose this opportunity – she might not have another one and she didn't want to grow old alone.

After a few months Nikoly moved in and Maria now had a stepfather as well as another room mate, as her grandmother now had to share her and her sister's room. For a while everything seemed perfect and they were a happy family until just after the collapse of the Soviet Union. It was 1991, Maria had just turned eleven and her stepfather returned from work earlier than usual drunk and rambling and swearing and cursing having just lost his job. The factory where he worked was marked for privatisation and he was no longer needed. Maria never remembered her real father or his drunkenness, but deep in the recesses of her sub-conscious mind her stepfather's drunkenness instilled a fear in Maria – a fear of something she somehow recognised and understood.

Maria's mother wasn't yet home from work and Maria and her sister hid in their room as her stepfather swore and cursed at their grandmother, who tried her best to calm him for the sake of the girls. From that day forward there would be many days when he would come home drunk. He would have spells of sobriety, sometimes weeks when he would focus himself on making his way round the various factories and industrial plants looking for work, but increasingly as he was turned away he turned more and more to drink. His rage and anger grew, as did his deepening hatred of the new government and sadness and despair at the collapse of the old Soviet Union. At least under the old Administration he would never have been out of work, there was always a job for him and there was always food on the table. As a party member he was valued under the Soviet Government, but now he was no one, nothing. It seemed no one cares for anyone apart from themselves.

Although he never hit Maria or her sister, there were times when he did hit Maria's mother, normally when she was trying to calm him or sober him up. He would occasionally shove her hard up against a wall, or throw her to the floor, or slap her hard across the face. Sometimes, when they were alone together in their bedroom he would aggressively force himself upon her. Maria would hear her mother's sobs and cries of stop, which were always ignored.

During times of abstinence her stepfather would recognize what he had done and ask for forgiveness, with promises that he would never behave like that again. In between his bouts of drunkenness they would be fairly happy. They would go to the park or take a boat on the lake, go to the cinema or take a stroll in the forest when he would always demand that he push Maria's wheelchair because of the difficult terrain. He would be like any other devoted father until his search for work commenced and the refusals followed one after another, and the bottle reappeared.

Chapter 4

Kidnapped

It was early evening midway through the summer. Maria, her sister and a few friends were sitting lazily on the grass watching everyone wander around. It was warm and sunny, the air smelt of freshly cut grass and everyone felt relaxed and comfortable and enjoying the first festival of the year. When summers arrive in that part of Siberia the whole world seems to instantly change around them. Flowers, almost overnight, suddenly bloom into every conceivable shape and color, the green of the trees shine and dance magically against the burning sun and birds frantically dart around, making as much noise as possible, as though they knew they didn't have long and should make the most of it.

Butterflies gently fluttered over the heads of everyone sitting on the grass boarders which separate the flower beds and pathways as Maria sat on the blanket with her friends laughing and chatting about all the things teenagers generally chat about. She had just turned seventeen, had posters of pop groups on her bedroom walls and teen magazines under her bed. She thought of romance and whispered and giggled as good-looking boys of her own age passed where they were sitting. She leant back against the wheel of her wheelchair, which was just behind her, gazed up at the clear evening sky and wondered what it would be like kissing a boy for the very first time. The great thing about Siberian evenings is that is doesn't get dark until well past midnight and the sky remains clear and blue and the sun shines until very late. Maria stared up at the noisy birds racing overhead and imagined herself in the arms of a boy.

Something caught her attention and brought her back down to earth. She watched as a group of teenage boys settled themselves on the grass across the path directly in front of where Maria and her friends were sitting. The four boys were drinking beer, laughing loudly and play-fully pushing and taunting one another as they sat themselves down, gazing over to where the girls were sitting. She didn't recognize any of the boys accept the tallest – she had noticed him wondering around the village square earlier. She had thought he looked nice and giggled with her sister as he passed close by. He seemed to stand out from the others, tall, handsome, lovely eyes and a lovely warm smile. She stared at him as he fooled around with the other boys, stealing an occasional glance over to where Maria was sitting. And every time he did she blushed and turned away, towards her sister and friends, pretending to have been listening to what they were saying. Her sister saw a friend from school walking with her mother in the distance across the small square. Jumping up she turned to Maria and promised she would be back in a minute and raced off towards them. Maria watched as her sister rushed up behind her friend grabbing her by the shoulder. Her friend turned abruptly and they both burst out laughing as she recognised who had made her jump. She watched as her sister greeted her friend's mother and then, tucking her arms round her friend's, resumed walking with them and away from Maria. Maria looked towards the boy again. She seemed fixated – it was hard to keep her eyes off him. Maria had tried to avoid all thoughts of boys and relationships and love, she knew that being an invalid with no legs nobody would ever like her, let alone want to date and kiss her. The growing woman inside her yearned for affection and love and warmth but she fought her inner feelings and desires and tried to understand who she was and what she was and believed that no one would ever want her in any romantic way.

But as she stared at him he kept staring back at her. She turned and looked around to see if perhaps he was actually smiling at someone else, perhaps someone prettier nearby, but there was no one apart from her and her friends, and he definitely wasn't looking at any of them. "He is beautiful and he's looking straight at me," she thought to herself as she gazed at him. She didn't turn away but, as he smiled at her, found herself smiling back. Her heart raced as she watched him get up, bend to whisper something to one of his friends who nodded and smiled back to him, and walk over to where they were sitting. By the time he was standing over her looking down, she felt as though she was going to explode.

"I'm Sergey," he said crouching, offering his hand. Her friends had suddenly fallen silent and stared up at him. "Hello, I'm Maria," they giggled as she shook his hand. She stared at him thinking how wonderful he was and imagined herself being whisked off to a faraway fairytale land.

"I work over at the tracks," he said pointing to the rail station which was just a short walk from the village square. "I am going to meet some friends there in a minute, why don't you come with us?"

"I can't," she said but thinking to herself how much she would love to and that, at that moment in time, she would probably go anywhere and do anything he wanted. Never had a boy asked her to join him, and she still wasn't sure this was happening. It seemed like a dream, a surreal fantasy that you somehow felt wasn't possible but seemed so true.

"Why not?" he asked and looked around at her friends who whispered and giggled quietly amongst themselves.

She didn't know what to say.

"Come on," he looked at her chair, "it isn't far and we won't be long. Can I push you?" She so desperately wanted to go with him, to feel what it was like being with a boy for the first time. Maybe, just maybe she might even kiss him.

"I can manage myself," she said, almost confirming that she would go with him.

"But I want to," he said. He seemed so kind, so sensitive, so reassuring. "Here, let me lift you, don't worry," he laughed, "I won't drop you."

He gently picked her up and placed her in her chair as her friends stared, silent, and dumbstruck.

"You promise we won't be long? My sister will be back and I don't want her to worry."

"I promise." He said

"Tell Nadezhda I won't be long," Maria said to her friends smiling as she was pushed away. They nodded and smiled and giggled excitedly and thought how wonderful it was that Maria had met a boy, and what a boy!

Sergey waved to his friends across the pavement and wheeled Maria onto the path and away from the square towards the rail track.

"Promise we won't be long?" Maria looked up and over her shoulder, concerned yet smiling, anxious and nervous yet extremely excited.

"I promise, you can meet my friends, stay a short while, have a beer or two and I will take you back."

She had never drunk a beer in her life, let alone two. What an evening this was going to be, she thought to herself as he pushed her nearer to the tracks and the trains.

"Where do you live?" she asked.

"In Tumen," he said. "I work on the trains. We take freight backwards and forwards, and to other places too. I have been all over the region. All over. I am going home later, on the last train. On that train there," he pointed towards a line of four freight carriages sitting quietly on the tracks. She wondered if she should tell him that her grandmother came from Tumen, but decided against it – she was sure he wasn't interested in where her grandmother came from!

They left the noise and activity of the village square and made their way towards the row of carriages he had pointed at a few moments earlier. "My friends are having a few beers in one of the middle carriages. We'll take the train and empty carriages back to Tumen tonight and we'll fill them with goods and stuff first thing tomorrow morning and take them someplace else. It is an easy job really." She was feeling a bit uneasy with being so far from her friends and her sister, but felt good about being with Sergey, the only boy she had ever been alone with. She sat and listened to him as he chatted about his job and the goods they transported from town to town and the fact that sometimes crates would break open and they managed to take some of the goods home. It wasn't stealing he said, "because they broke and things fell out". Sometimes there would be parts for cars, which he managed to sell to a local market or wood or coal.

As they approached the carriages they could hear voices and laughter.

"Hey guys, it's me Sergey," Sergey called up as they moved towards the centre carriages. The third carriage's sliding door was half open and a head appeared round the corner. "Hey, Sergey, where have you been? Who's your friend?" he asked as he stood in the doorway.

"Maria," he called back, "Give me a hand."

The other boy jumped down off the carriage and together they lifted Maria out of the chair and onto the carriage. A girl appeared "Hi Maria," she said looking down at Maria as she sat and waited for Sergey and his friend to lift her chair into the carriage. They then lifted her back into her chair and wheeled her across to the far corner of the carriage, where everyone was sitting on wooden boxes or on the floor leaning against the carriage walls. Apart from the girl that had just greeted her, Maria noticed one other girl and apart from Sergey and his friend, two other boys. Maria said hello to everyone and Sergey handed her a beer. As everyone around her chatted and laughed she stared at Sergey as he talked with his friends and drank his beer. The compartment was warm and cozy and everyone seemed friendly and kind and she was getting drunker and drunker. She had never been drunk before, nor had she ever been in such a place before. She liked the effect the beers were having, and she loved being there – listening to everyone laughing and watching as they too seemed to get drunk and noisy and less inhibited. She looked at Sergey and he occasionally looked back at her and smiled. She was enjoying every minute and she never felt better in her life. Suddenly the train jolted and moved and a wave of panic spread over her.

"What is happening?" she called out.

"We are going home," one of the boys whose name she couldn't remember shouted drunkenly and laughed.

"But I can't, let me off," she half called, half giggled through the fuzzy mist of intoxication.

"You can't get off now," the boy said, "We are moving," and laughed some more. She looked around trying to find Sergey. It was dark and now very late and through the haze she just made out Sergey kissing one of the girls.

Everyone was drunk and ignoring her calls to be let off the train.

"Sergey, help me, please," she pleaded. Sergey looked over. "Don't worry, we will be returning shortly and we'll let you off when we get back. There is nothing you can do now so have another beer," and he handed her his half empty bottle. Tears were rolling down her eyes as she uneasily sipped the beer.

She woke up and everything around her was silent. The train had stopped. She looked about – there was nobody. The carriage was empty apart from discarded beer bottles and cigarette ends and a girl's scarf. She looked around for her wheelchair but that was gone too. Using her arms to lever herself upright, she slowly crawled to the carriage door, which was slightly open, but not enough to get out. Wedging her small body up against the metal surround, she pushed the heavy sliding door inch by inch until it was opened just enough for her squeeze her body through. She perched at the edge of the doorway looking down at the ground about six feet below. Once more tears filled her eyes. Somehow she could sense that things were changing. She missed her sister and her friends and wanted to be back with them laughing on the grass and looking at the boys walking by. Why did she allow herself go off with him, a complete stranger? She thought about her sister and friends and wondered how they would be worrying and looking everywhere for her. She had never gone off on her own before. She thought about her poor lovely grandmother who must be beside herself with worry by now. She could see her mother banging on the door of the local police station waking the sleepy and probably drunk officer in charge, demanding that a search party be sent for. There was only one policeman in her village and he had little to do and even if he wanted to there was no way he would ever be able to summon other policemen in the middle of the night from other villages and towns nearby.

And anyway, she was last seen going off with a boy. He would probably tell her mother to go back home as her daughter was sure to be having a good time somewhere and would be back with the morning sun.

She looked out of the carriage. Where was she anyway? She could see a few sets of tracks in front of her, a solitary carriage further up to her right, on another track, and forest as far as she could see in both directions.

She leaned out as far as she could and could just about make out the end of the line of carriages in both directions, but no engine. Whatever had moved them earlier that night had been detached and had disappeared. She had no idea what time it was or how long she had been asleep but she thought it might have been at least a couple of hours as it was just getting light, and mornings start very early in the summer in Siberia. She knew she had to get off the train as it might leave again and take her god only knows where, so she rolled herself onto her stomach and slowly swung her body over the edge of the doorway. Gripping the bottom of the doorframe tightly, she swung her body over the edge. Maria hung there for a few seconds, looked down, closed her eyes and let herself drop, screaming in agony as the stumps of her legs smashed against the hard ground below.

She lay on the ground, still, eyes tightly closed, moaning with the agony and shock of the fall. As the pain gradually subsided she slowly pulled herself up, propping herself upright with her arms. She looked around and under the train and saw a flicker of light in a clearing, between other carriages and across a few more sets of tracks. Although there was room for her small body to go between the wheels under the train, she was afraid that she might get stuck, or that the train might move, so she slowly crawled alongside the line of carriages to the end and across the tracks towards the flickering light. The ground was hard and stony and her hands soon became cut and bruised as she moved them forward a few inches, raising her torso slightly with her shoulders and swinging her body forward. She grimaced each time the ends of her bruised stumps touched the ground.

As she got closer to the flickering light she could see it was a small fire, and around the fire a group of people were huddled. Behind them stood an old dilapidated two story building. She could see the broken windows and door, half hanging on one hinge. Even though it was getting lighter, she couldn't quite make out the exact number of people but it looked as though there were also a few lying curled up on the floor, probably asleep. She could see, however, that they were not the group that had left her in the carriage but looked like some of the homeless she sometimes saw begging in the streets of her village. She hadn't seen them often, as they quickly moved on, but she knew they did exist. She was afraid, afraid of where she was and of the group huddled in front of her, but she knew she had to get help and they were probably the only people that could help her. She slowly and nervously made her way towards them.

As she approached one of them looked up and stared at her. He didn't say anything, just stared at her as she shuffled closer. He silently nodded, as though accepting she was one of them, and bowed his head again, going back into his own world.

"Hello, can you help me?" Maria whispered to no one in particular.

No one replied. No one looked up. One of them slouched drunkenly to the floor, curled up, muttered something and fell asleep. The others just sat there staring at the fire, occasionally taking sips from bottles by their side or in their hands, occasionally muttering something incomprehensible.

"Can you help me, please?" Maria pleaded, louder.

The person that first stared at her looked up and said "We can't help anybody." He looked back down at the bottle in his hand and took a swig.

"But I need to get home to my village, I fell asleep on the carriage, over there," she pleaded, pointing to where she had come from, but no one was looking, "and I want to get back home, please help."

Staring at his bottle he said quietly "we can't help you, what can we do?"

"Where are we? Where is the nearest village?" she said, trying to hold back her tears.

"That way," he said pointing "About two kilometres."

"Two kilometres!" she screamed to herself. It had taken all her energy and willpower just to crawl from the train over to where the homeless were huddled – she knew she couldn't crawl two kilometres.

"Best you rest and see what the day brings," he said, laying down and falling instantly asleep. She curled up in front of the dying embers of the fire and closed her eyes. Afraid to go to sleep but exhausted, she lay listening to the silence around her, hearing nothing but the crackle of the fire and occasional snores of the homeless.

She looked up at the clear sky and the clouds and watched as the birds swooped and squawked. She could hear her mother in the kitchen talking to her sister, she felt the familiar warmth of her apartment and smelt its recognizable smell, a smell so distinctive and comforting. She opened her eyes and stared up and watched as the clouds turned dark and filled the sky above her and the noise of the birds turned to a crunch and grind and rattle and clash of metal hitting metal.

"What have we got here?" a voice said from above as the clouds turned to a dark human shape staring down at her.

She propped herself upright, frightened, staring up at the old man standing in front of her and then around at the tracks as she saw an engine coupling the solitary carriage in the distance.

"Can *you* help me?" she asked urgently.

"I can't even help myself, my dear," he said, "but I do have some bread you can share. I don't have much." He handed her a small piece of bread and sat down beside her looking out at the tracks.

"You don't look like one of us," he said, looking at Maria's clean and relatively new clothing and down at the recognizable stumps of her legs beneath her blue jeans.

Maria quickly told him the story and how she ended up on the carriage in the middle of the night alone.

He shrugged "Shit happens," he said and laughed to himself, "one minute all is fine, next minute shit happens. The best thing for you to do is to try and get the attention of one of the train drivers that turn up to pick up the carriages" he nodded at the engine towing a carriage off into the distance, "and find out if anything is going back to your village, although they rarely take any notice of us. The drivers are supposed to check all the carriages before they move them, but they rarely do. They don't care who's on board, as we get kicked off anyway when they come to load. Then who knows where we end up!" He laughed. "The village is quite a way down there," he pointed, and there is a phone box in the centre of the village, but mostly it doesn't work, or so they say. Does your mother have a phone?"

Maria shook her head. She didn't know anyone with a phone and only saw the headmistress use the phone once when she was in her office a couple of years ago, and even then she remembered that she couldn't get through to whoever it was she was calling.

"Where do you live?" she asked.

"Here and there. Nowhere really. We may go on the carriages somewhere," he nodded, speaking not about himself, but about the group. "Beg or steal food and, if lucky, come back here, or maybe end up somewhere else. We sometimes walk into the village, but they don't give much, the bigger towns are the best, but it is a long walk, about five kilometres that way," he pointed in the opposite direction. "The road is a hundred metres behind the building," he nodded at the building, "you might be able to stop a car or a cart, but they don't pass that frequently, one or two every hour or so. No, your best bet is to try and get the attention of an engine driver, and then he will tell you if and when a carriage is going back to your village. They pick up and drop off carriages all day. But you have to be quick." He looked down at Maria's stumps.

She noticed a couple of the homeless walking towards the carriages she had come from. "Where are they going?" she asked.

"They'll be off for a lift. They will wait in one of the carriages and go wherever it goes. There's no food sitting around here!" he laughed. She suddenly felt very hungry and quickly ate the bread.

Maria carefully tore strips from the bottom of her blouse and wrapped them around her sore and bruised hands. She also tied her trouser legs together just below the bottom of her stumps to make it more comfortable for her to move around. Her legs were sore and badly bruised but the rest of the morning she ignored the throbbing pain and crawled over the tracks towards engines that came and went, trying to shout up at the drivers who either ignored her or simply didn't see her. It crossed her mind about placing herself in the centre of the tracks directly in front of a train, but from the way the drivers seldom looked down or around she knew she would survive just enough time for the engine to run her over, and even then she doubted that the drivers would notice. The engines were monsters compared to her little body, and she simply wasn't quick enough to get to the drivers as they stopped and connected the carriages – by the time she got near them they were on their way again. Her hands were raw and bleeding and her arms ached terribly from the lifting and swinging of her body up and down and over the tracks. Once or twice the drivers seemed to notice her, seemed to hesitate for a few seconds, only to look up and pretend the shabby looking girl with no legs was not there or not real or some kind of decoy for a gang to board and steal his train. Evening arrived and the engines stopped coming and going and Maria returned to the huddle of homeless sitting round the seemingly endless fire. She hoped to see the familiar face of the old man she had spoken to earlier, but he was nowhere. New faces sat – some talking, some silent, some drinking, some sleeping but all hungry. She needed to eat but couldn't bear to ask for food, not from those whom she saw and knew were desperately hungry themselves. No one asked who she was or why she was there – they came and went, each with a story to tell but no one to tell it to.

She curled up silently, desperately hungry and thirsty and thinking about her sister and mother and grandmother. She fell into a deep sleep.

"Morning my dear," the same voice as yesterday said. "Here, you must be hungry, take this," and handed Maria a bottle of water, a chunk of black bread and three small apples. Her eyes lit up as she gulped down the water and stared at the apples and bread. Never in her life could she imagine the joy of being given an apple, not just one apple but three. She said nothing as she ate the bread and quickly followed by the three apples, one after another.

"Slow down little lady," the old man said, "you might not get any more for a while." She shrugged. She wasn't homeless, she would be going back home soon, back to her mother and grandmother, to sausages for breakfast and soup for dinner, to the sounds of laughter, to her room and her books and her posters and her sister's nagging yet funny ways. Soon she would be wearing clean clothes and have a hot bath and be able to clean her teeth. Soon she wouldn't have to go to the toilet round the back of old building where others had pissed and crapped, hoping no one would see her. She wasn't homeless.

"One of the advantages of living on the road," he chuckled as Maria finished the last apple, nibbling at every last possible morsel.

She wondered if she would ever think about this old man when she finally got home. She wondered about his story, why did he have no place to live, no family to look after him, why did he search the forest floor for apples when he should be sitting around a table with his sons or daughters, grandsons or granddaughters.

She heard the rumble of the first engine of the day rolling along the tracks.

"Thank you," she said, looking up at him.

"Good luck," he said and turned towards the forest. She watched as he slowly made his way over the tracks and disappeared between the trees. "Good luck too," she whispered as she made her way towards the approaching engine.

She sat directly in the middle of the open ground so she could see up and down the tracks for approaching engines. There were a few carriages scattered around, some solitary, others in chains of three or four or five. As she looked around she understood that fate was now asking her to seek rescue from the very machines that had originally altered her life. Trains had taken away an ordinary, normal existence and given her a life so very different and difficult. It was because of her accident twelve years ago that she was now clawing her way over the tracks in search of a train to take her back to normality.

The previous day Maria had noticed two carriages on the set of tracks closest to where everyone grouped. The two carriages sat on their own about fifty metres along the tracks from the fire. They had not moved nor been taken by the flow of engines coming and going throughout the day but seemed unused dilapidated passenger carriages. She could see the broken windows, shattered glass and graffiti. Intrigued and wondering whether it might be a safer and warmer place to sleep, she decided to take a closer look and slowly made her way across the tracks. She could see a few people still sleeping around the fire, even though it was almost mid-day and noticed two middle aged women standing chatting to each other. They didn't seem like the others she had met and seen – they wore cotton scarves round their heads and shawls over their shoulders. They looked out of place but Maria didn't think anything of it, this was a strange place.

As she made her way towards the run-down carriages two men appeared from inside the dilapidated building near to where everyone sat huddled every night, ducking under the half attached door. They stood and watched Maria as she swung her little body backwards and forwards over the tracks towards the two carriages.

Maria looked up at the broken windows and mangled metal doorframe in front of her and smelt the smell of urine and excrement. No wonder nobody slept here, she thought. As she turned to leave she was startled by the two men standing behind her. She suddenly became very frightened, but struggled not to show it.

"What are you doing here?" the taller of the two asked menacingly. The men looked really rough – she had never seen men looking like this before. Both unshaved with greasy, dirty shoulder length hair and dirty clothes. She could smell them too. They didn't smell like the other homeless, but they smelt unwashed and of stale beer and cigarettes and vodka.

Even from where she was looking up at him she could smell the taller one's foul breath and could see his stained, dirty teeth through his evil grin. The tall one had a jagged scar that ran from the corner of his right eye to the centre of his cheek and his left eye was permanently half closed. The shorter one stood slightly behind the taller one, and just stared at her.

"You are a fucking bitch whore, fucking those scumbags for a bit of food." Maria froze, terrified. "Now you can do it for free." The tall man grabbed her hair and pulled her onto her back towards the open door of the carriage.

"Let her be," she heard the other man say, tugging on the tall mans dirty coat.

"None of your fucking business," he snarled back and shrugged him off.

Maria tried to scream but he punched her hard in the mouth, splitting her lip and sending her into unconsciousness.

She awoke to the stench of the man's breath breathing over her. She was lying on her back on the floor of the carriage, her arms were above her head and she could hear the buckle of the belt being undone. She opened her eyes to see the top of his head as he looked down to where he was trying to force himself onto her. She looked above her head and saw fragments of glass. Grabbing the largest piece she could find, she screamed and, as he looked up, thrust a jagged piece of glass into his face.

He fell backwards, clutching at his wound as blood spurted through his fingers, over Maria. She turned over and scrabbled desperately along the floor, over the pools of urine, and broken glass and through open connecting carriage doors, falling and wedging herself between the metal connectors of the two carriages.

She listened as he screamed. She could hear him trying to get up from the floor. She heard the other man's voice from outside the carriage, probably keeping guard, and could hear him jump up into the carriage. "Find her," the tall man screamed. She was almost sick with fear as she heard his footsteps approach the connecting doors. She looked up and saw him peering down at her tiny frail body jammed up against the metal supports, at her frightened eyes staring back at him, pleading with him. "Please," she whispered.

He stared down at her for a few seconds and then turned and called "She's not here, she must have disappeared out the other way."

"Take me to a fucking hospital," the tall man screamed.

She listened as the two men fumbled out of the carriage, one supporting the other. Maria vomited.

She was stuck. Her arms and shoulders were wedged between the metal supports and, as she tried to wiggle herself free, she slipped down even more, lodging herself tighter. She could hear the sounds of the engines coming and going over the tracks, the metal clunks as freight carriages were joined together and to the engines, and the roar of diesel as they moved off with their new loads, but no voices. She was frightened of calling out, just in case they were out there waiting for her. She felt sure that, at some point, they would come back to take their revenge. Time passed, minutes, hours. The evening drew in, the engines stopped coming.

She wondered if she would die there in that tiny corner, unable to move. Would the old man who had given her bread and apples come looking for her? He would probably think that she had managed to get a carriage back to her village. Just as she started to shiver with the change of temperature as the evening drew in, she suddenly heard the sound of two women talking quietly to themselves. She stopped breathing and listened, the voices, although faint and whisper-like, seemed to be getting closer.

"Hello!" she shouted. The voices stopped. "Hello, please help me!" she shouted again and the voices started up again, but louder and rushing towards her.

"Hello, I am in here, help me, I am stuck," Maria called.

"Where are you?" one of the women called, walking along the carriage.

"Here, in between the two carriages."

"Oh my goodness," said one woman peering over the couplings into the gap where Maria was wedged. "Let's see if we can get you out of here." One of the women rushed round the carriage to the opposite side behind Maria, leant over and tried to hook her arms under Maria's shoulders, while the other pulled Maria from the front. Maria cried out as the metal scraped against her torso.

"Oh, you poor dear, lets get you cleaned up." The two ladies placed Maria on the ground and wiped her dried blood and vomit stained mouth with a rag. Maria looked up at the two women fussing over her and recognised them as the two women that were near the fire earlier that day. "We have got to get you into some other clothes," said the other lady fiddling with Maria's torn and dirty jacket. She took off her shawl and placed it around Maria's shoulders. "I want to go home," Maria whispered, she was too shocked and tired to say anything else.

"Don't worry dear, we'll get you home," Maria collapsed.

Maria woke to the rocking of the train.

"There dear, have some of this," said the lady offering her a cup of warm team poured from an old tatty looking flask. Maria pulled herself up just enough to take a few sips of the sweet hot tea, and fell back down again. She looked up and saw the two women faces looking over her. She could hardly keep her eyes open

"Where are we going?" Maria asked sleepily.

"To Moscow dear, we are going to Moscow."

Chapter 5

Moscow

Maria awoke to tugs on her arm. "Come on, we must leave now."

"Where are we going?" Maria asked as she followed the women to the sliding doors of the carriage. It had stopped. She heard loud banging on the wooden walls and shouts of "Get Off, Get Off."

The doors slid open and two railway workers shouted inside the carriage for everyone to get off. Maria looked around. Apart from the two women, there were three or four others in the same carriage. She watched as they hastily and silently gathered their meager things and jumped off the train. The two women clambered off and helped Maria down onto the ground below. "Hurry along," one of the women turned to her and said. Maria struggled to keep up with them as they rushed across the compound of the depot. Maria's hands were still raw and blistered and she grimaced every time she swung her body backwards and forwards. She glanced back at the train to see handfuls of people coming from almost every carriage.

"Come dear," said one of the women as she slipped easily between a large hole in the wire fence that surrounded the depot. Maria followed and the second woman followed Maria. They crossed a small desolate open area between two dilapidated buildings and out onto a small side street. They walked up the street to a junction and stood on the corner. The three of them waited. An hour passed, and then two. Maria was hungry and thirsty. Finally, after almost three hours of standing silently on that same street corner carefully watching every car that passed, an old Lada approached, slowed down and stopped on the corner in front of the three of them. A disheveled dirty looking man driving the car leaned over and wound down the window.

"Get in," he said.

One of the ladies lifted Maria onto the back seat, closed the door and walked round the car, jumping in beside her while the other woman got into the front seat.

"Where are we going?" asked Maria.

"We are going home dear," the woman in the front replied.

"But this is not my home," Maria said "I don't understand."

"We saved you dear, didn't we? And we looked after you. Well, now you have to work for us for a little while and earn your fare back to your village."

Maria silently stared out of the grimy window as they drove along the outer suburbs of Moscow. This was not the beautiful grand city that she had dreamt about and seen on television. This was a deprived, desolate looking Moscow of grubby, dirty high-rise apartments. As she stared out of the grimy window she watched as small gangs of youths milled around street corners kicking cans and smoking, children searching in waste bins, wild dogs following pedestrians up and down the pavement hoping for a morsel or scrap and solitary beggars standing, heads bowed, arms outstretched. She looked at the graffiti on the walls and run down decrepit kiosks. Old men and women sat or stood in front of a few packets of cigarettes, or mangy looking fruit and vegetables, or odds and sods from their home laid out neatly on dirty handkerchiefs on the ground hoping for a few roubles.

This was not the Moscow of her dreams, but a city of poverty and deprivation and solitude. This was the capital of her country, a country that once she was led to believe was the best, the most powerful and the most wonderful place to live in the world.

They pulled up outside a large metal graffiti covered gate secured by a thick padlock. The gate was set between barbed wire topped walls in the middle of two run down empty boarded up buildings. The driver got out, unlocked the padlock and swung the double gates open. He jumped back into the car, placing the big chunky padlock in his lap, drove through the opening, jumped back out and closed and padlocked the gate behind them.

"Home dear."

They lifted Maria out of the car. Maria stared at the dilapidated, ramshackle building in front of them. "Tomorrow you will start work, and we will get you something to get around on. Oh, and don't think about running away dear, you have nowhere to go." She beckoned Maria to follow them over to the building, Maria following behind, gingerly placing her hands onto the ground, between shards of broken glass, old cans, waste paper, sticks and stones. The driver unlocked the thick heavy door to the building and she followed them inside.

She looked around at the gloomy room and at the people laying or sitting or chatting. In one corner she noticed a large two ringed stove where soup was being cooked and the room smelt of cabbage and dirty human bodies. The walls were bare apart from some old tatty clothes hanging in one corner, perhaps drying, and a couple of torn paper pictures of places Maria didn't recognize. As they entered, the room fell silent and everyone looked up at the women and Maria.

"This is Maria," the lady called, "make her feel welcome."

"Maria, this is now your home. We will come to collect you tomorrow morning, the others will show you around. There is food and some blankets in the corner over there and we will bring you some new clothing in the morning. You will just have to make do tonight I am afraid dear. Don't worry, you will be all right. We are not bad people, just work hard for us dear and you can go home."

Maria started at everyone staring silently back at her. The two women turned and left, locking the door behind them. Maria covered her face with her hands and burst out crying.

"There, there, it will be all right, come, have some soup, you must be very hungry," she looked up as a woman similar to her grandmother, with a kind homely face, put her arm around Maria's shoulder. Someone else put her arm round her other shoulder, a young girl, just a little older than Maria, with a dark wine-red birthmark covering almost all of her face. She wiped the tears from her eyes and looked across the room. An old man sat on a wooden crate with a pair of old crutches leaning up against the wall behind him, she could see an empty trouser leg. He was talking to another man, a tiny deformed man sitting on the floor. Another couple of elderly women sat huddled together on the floor chatting.

Two days ago Maria was sitting happily on the grass in her village watching as everyone strolled by and now she was being held prisoner in a squalid building with the deformed and the elderly. She couldn't stop her tears. She cried for her mother and her grandmother, she cried for her sister, for her school and for her room with her posters and books. As she cried the girl and old lady sat quietly either side, with their arms holding her tightly, comforting her, reassuring her. She cried and cried and cried until there were no tears left.

Later that evening, when Maria had no more tears, and after she had managed to eat a little soup and bread, the old lady, whose name she now knew was Olga, and Svetlana, the girl with the birthmark, explained the rules and described the work Maria would be doing.

Olga told Maria that every morning they are all taken to a Metro station where they worked begging for the gypsies. This was all arranged with the local mafia gangs who ran the streets and the Metro throughout Moscow. These small Mafia groups extorted money from street vendors, kiosk owners and beggars within their territory. To operate you had to pay, there was no question of not paying. These were ruthless people in a harsh hard world and their living was the "commission" they made on the money earned on their territory. Not paying, or failing to pay the correct amount usually resulted in a beating. A light beating at first, as a warning, and a more severe beating should that warning not be heeded. The gypsies paid the local Mafia a set fee for each beggar that they had under their control.

From seven am until seven pm every single day they would beg. With no papers or documents they couldn't go to the police, nor run away, and anyway, the local police are paid by the mafia.

The gypsies have to pay the mafia every day so if they are late for "work" or don't turn up, or leave their spot without permission they are severely punished. The gypsies keep a very close eye on them all. They come round and collect the money several times during the day and at the end of every day. Punishment is generally a beating by one of the men. "We don't see the men that often," Olga said, "only when they come round to collect the money, or pick us up or drop us off. Generally we are dropped off at the Metro up the road and we make our own way to our Metro station but if we are late we are beaten. We cannot ever beg on the Metro trains ourselves, firstly it is too dangerous as there are police everywhere and the gypsies don't pay *them*, and anyway, other mafia groups run the Metro trains. If we ever get stopped and the gypsies have to pay the police to get us released, we have to make up the money begging harder and longer hours. We are not allowed to talk to anyone for long – if we are caught talking for too long we are warned and then if we continue we're punished. Also, if we are found with any money on us after we have finished for the day we are also punished. The gypsies are suspicious of everyone and everything."

"What punishment?" Maria asked

"We are beaten." Svetlana replied

"They beat *you*?" Maria asked, looking at Olga, wondering how anyone could beat an old lady, or a disabled man, but she quickly recalled being punched in the face and almost raped and understood that yes it was possible, that these people were inhuman.

"Yes, they will beat you. They won't beat your face, as you couldn't work with bruises and cuts to your face, but they will beat your body so badly that you might not be able to walk or breath properly for days. If they beat you so bad that you couldn't work, as soon as you are able you have to make up the money and work harder and longer." Maria couldn't believe what she heard. Was this really happening?

"I was once beaten because I bought an ice cream," said the man with one leg who had wondered over to them. "I was tired and thinking about my granddaughter, I though about how she used to eat her ice cream and play in the park. I just fancied one myself, that was all. And I was beaten. They said it wasn't my money I had spent, it was theirs and therefore I was stealing from them. So be very very careful."

"Who beat you?" Maria asked.

"One of the women, just to humiliate me more. She punched me in my ribs, slapped my face, pulled my hair, and kicked me when I fell."

"Don't you have family, friends that can help, that can rescue you?"

"The only friends we have are here, in this room. My son was killed in Afghanistan, my wife died of cancer. They both died within six months of each other. My granddaughter went to live in the Ukraine with her mother I sold the papers to my apartment for two cases of vodka when times were bad and when I couldn't cope with my loss. We all have a story to tell, we are all here for a reason, and we all have nowhere to go."

"I was sold to the gypsies by my stepfather," Svetlana said. "My mother had gone to live in America with another man. She ran off. My stepfather didn't want me around any more. After my mother left he started to drink heavily. He soon lost his job because he was always late to work and often drunk. He knew someone that knew someone. I was sold, for how much I don't know, and was told I have to work to pay them back. I have been here for six months, it isn't too bad in the summer but the winter is bad. You get so cold." Maria sat numbed as she listened to their stories.

Olga met the gypsies when she was already on the streets. She was sleeping in a derelict building near to where she used to live, along with others who, like her, had nowhere else to go. It was autumn, the nights were getting colder and they all somehow knew they would never survive the winter – they would all be dead by the first fall of snow. Her only son had grown up and had long since moved out, making money in some business or other, she never knew what he did but the last time she saw him, almost two years ago, he turned up outside her apartment in a big new expensive looking black car which looked very out of place amongst the shabbiness of their run-down apartment block.

She watched from the kitchen window of her third floor apartment. She liked to sit watching the world below – she had little else to do in her life. She would sip hot tea and watch as people came and went, or stood chatting to one another. In the summer she would watch as the children played in the small courtyard below and in the winter she would watch the snow fall and people scurry back and forth. People stared as he got out of his big car, his driver standing nearby smoking. She watched him as he walked across the courtyard and into the entrance directly below. She walked over to the front door, opening it for him as he emerged from the elevator. He didn't stay long, just made an excuse that he was passing and thought he would pop in to say hello. They had nothing to say to each other. He asked how she was, she said okay, she asked how he was, he said fine, and that was about it. Although he was her son she no longer had anything to share with him and he had nothing to say to her. After a few minutes he made his excuses and left. She went back to her kitchen window and watched as he walked back across the courtyard. The driver saw him coming, stubbed out his cigarette and opened the car door for him. He got in, not even looking up. That was the last time she saw him.

About a year ago she had a knock on the door. As usual she had sat by the kitchen window, sipping black tea, watching the world go by. She noticed three strange looking people in black leather jackets walk from the apartment block opposite, across the courtyard and into her apartment block, but thought nothing of it. One of them had a black briefcase, and another was talking on a mobile phone. An hour had passed and there was a knock on the door. She walked over the door and peered through the spy hole. There was a man standing smiling, knowing she was looking at him. He was on his own, he held up a badge, but she could not make it out and so she opened the door slightly. He introduced himself as Alex from some company to do with property, but she didn't understand. He said he had a proposition for her, which would give her a little extra money to buy some nice things for herself and perhaps for the apartment. As he looked around he said it could do with a little renovation. She didn't have much, a table and one rickety chair in the kitchen, a fridge and a two ringed hob. She had a bed, blankets, she couldn't afford sheets and often slept in her clothes, and a small sideboard where a couple of old photos were balanced. If she would sign the documents to her apartment over to him, she would be paid two thousand dollars – a huge amount of money. But don't worry, he said time and time again, the apartment would still be hers and she could always live in it until she died, but when she died, and god forbid it wouldn't be for years, he said, instead of the apartment going back to the corrupt government, it would be given to someone else, probably also elderly that needed somewhere to live. Did she have anyone who she would want to leave the apartment to? He asked. She had nobody. Apart from her, no one was registered at her apartment and so, when she died, she knew it would indeed go back to the government, a government she now hated. The old times were the best, she said to the man sitting next to her, nodding. Bring back the Communists, she said, much better for everyone. He nodded, agreeing with her. He took some papers from his brief case and asked her to sign them. Complicated legal jargon, he said, it just means that the papers to the apart-

ment would be signed to him and that she could continue
to live there – see, he said, showing her a separate piece of
paper. It all looked confusing to her, so she signed and
handed him the documents to the apartment. He said he
would be back in a few days with the money. They shook
hands and he left.

Her head was in the clouds. She wondered what she was
going to do with two thousand dollars. Two thousand
dollars!!! It was almost five years pension from the government. She couldn't believe her good fortune. She might
buy a nice chair to sit on, and perhaps a television. She
would love a television, but she had no idea what they
cost. She would certainly buy some new blankets and
sheets for the bed and a couple of nice dresses for herself.
She could not remember the last time she bought anything
for herself.

She sat by the window for the next two days waiting for
that kind man to turn up with her money. Two days passed
and no sign of him, three days, a week, two weeks then
suddenly there was a knock on the door. She looked
through the spy hole to see two policemen standing at her
door. Oh my goodness, she thought, something had happened to her son. She quickly opened the door. Behind the
two police man were two other men.

"Mrs. Olga Kimovich?" one of the policemen asked

"Yes," she replied

"You must leave the property immediately, this instant.
This is no longer your property and you are living here ille-
gally. You must pack your bags now and leave."

She almost collapsed, and steadied herself against the
door frame. She didn't understand. She tried to explain
what had happened. The policeman listened and asked for
the documents to her apartment.

She didn't have them. "We have the documents here,"
one of the men standing behind the policeman said "this is

our property." The policeman looked at the documents and did what they were paid to do, acknowledge that her name was not on the documents that she had signed the documents over to the property company. She was therefore no longer the legal owner and had to leave immediately.

"I am not leaving," she screamed and tried to close the door. The police brushed past her and into the apartment, while the two men grabbed Olga and pulled her out into the corridor. She fell to the floor screaming and crying. The men threw what few possessions she had out of the window onto the courtyard below, smashing the table and chair and sideboard. Her clothes fell here and there. People just stood and stared.

For a few hours she lay in the corridor, sobbing, not knowing what to do or where to go. She was frightened of the men in black leather jackets who had boarded and sealed the door to her apartment while she lay sobbing nearby. She could not go to the police either. She crawled outside to where her things lay smashed and broken. All her clothes were gone, they had been stolen while she lay in the corridor, and most of the wood from the broken furniture had also been taken. There was almost nothing left.

She walked aimlessly for a while, until she passed the shell of building "Twelve" which had been empty and in ruins for years. The place stunk, windows were smashed. A notice on the half open door read "Do Not Enter" but evening was approaching and she had no where else to go. The corridor was strewn with debris and litter and broken bottles, the remaining few floor tiles were smashed and the cracked walls were sprayed with graffiti. Building "Twelve" was once a smart local government office, but now an empty ransacked squalid shelter for the homeless, drunks and gangs of youths sniffing glue. She was scared as she gingerly made her way down the corridor, looking into the empty, stinking, filthy rooms. The third room she saw what looked like an old man huddled in a makeshift bed of newspaper and card, with an empty bottle of vodka next to him. She went into the room and huddled against the wall opposite. The first night she shook with fear and cold and thought she would die. The second day she spent rummaging through dustbins and behind the market stalls looking for anything she could eat. She drank the leftovers in cans and picked at the scraps of bread and fruit. The second night she wished she would die. She slept in the same corner in the same room with the same drunk curled up in the same opposite corner. That night a group of youths, high on glue, ran screaming and shouting throughout the building, jumping over and kicking a second man sleeping in the corridor just outside.

The third day she didn't move. She was so cold and so frightened. As evening drew nearer she heard the calls of a woman, asking if there was anyone inside. She summed up enough energy to shout out and a woman appeared from round the corner.

"Oh my," another woman followed behind, bending over Olga as she trembled with cold and fear. "Let us get you a hot bowl of soup and somewhere to stay, you can't stay here, it isn't safe." They helped her up, "come with us, we can help you." Olga was carefully ushered outside and into a waiting car. She was driven to an apartment about an hour away and that evening she was given hot soup and an old mattress to sleep on. The next morning she was told to have a bath and was given clean clothes. Two gypsy women came to the apartment and spoke in hushed voices to the two women that had rescued Olga from near death. Cash was exchanged and she was taken away.

"And here I am now," Olga said. "There is nowhere for me to go."

The man with no arms walked over and sat in front of Maria. "We all have a story to tell. They called me Stumpy at school, although I didn't go to school often," he laughed. "My mother, you see, was an alcoholic and I spent most of the time trying to look after her. She started drinking as soon as I was born, as soon as I was placed into her arms. Apparently she screamed with shock at her little baby boy with stumps for arms. She wouldn't have anything to do with me at first. The nurses looked after me, until she was eventually forced out of hospital and had to return home. She was repulsed by me. My earliest memories are of her face and disgust every time she looked my way. I don't suppose she believed that she could give birth to such a monster. My father was worse, apparently he drank before I was born and I made him worse, he wanted nothing to do with me. When he was drunk he would trip me up, laughing as I fell, knowing I was unable to break my fall or he would tell me to do something he knew I couldn't do, simply things like undoing a jam jar. He detested me and hated my drunken mother. He beat me a few times, but beat my mother more, blaming her for not giving him a "normal" son. He eventually left us when I was about seven.

"I had few friends. No one wanted to be friends with a cripple. I spent most of my time sitting alone on the doorstep dreaming of better things – a family that cared, a school that I enjoyed going to, friends to play with and of course I dreamt about what it would be like to have arms. I imagined myself climbing and swimming and riding a bike and playing ball – all the things normal people can do with a normal body. But I eventually learned to cope, although some of the private things were pretty hard to deal with, you know, going to the toilet and stuff, but I coped.

"My mother lost her job because of her drinking. She would never wake up on time and I frequently had to drag her out of bed and force her to work, but after a while I just couldn't be bothered and she became later and later, and skipped more and more days until one day she turned up for work three hours late and half drunk. She was told that she no longer had a job. I was blamed of course, for not waking her up on time. She screamed and shouted and threw things at me and slapped me a good few times around the face. She wished she had a normal child.

"One day I was in central Moscow for Victory Day and I was sitting watching the parade. I was only about sixteen years old, I was on my own and had stolen the fare from my mother's purse as she lay snoring. I tried to ware baggy shirts and things, you know, to hide the fact I had no arms, but sometimes it is almost impossible to hide, especially when I have to go onto the Metro, open doors, etc. The gypsies told me later that they had spotted me on my own buying a Metro ticket and keeping it in my mouth as I fed it through the turnstiles. They had followed me to the centre of Moscow and stood beside me as I watched the parade. It was great fun and I had a good day away from my drunken mother. To be honest I didn't want the day to end. I was anonymous. Sure, some people noticed I didn't have arms and sometimes children pointed or whispered to their mothers, but no one said anything to me and there was no drunken mother to look after. It got darker and later and I thought about going home, but I really didn't want to. Also, I was hungry, but I had no money. I had noticed a couple of beggars on the streets and then the thought struck me – I would beg for enough money to buy myself something to eat. I looked about, wondered over to a Metro and sat myself down just around the corner from the entrance. I rolled up the sleeves to my shirt, showing the stumps of my arms and, as people passed, asked for change. People started to put kopeks and roubles on the floor in front of me. As I looked down and mentally counted up the change I knew it wouldn't be long before I had enough money for some food and perhaps a can of coke. And then someone bent down and gathered up all the change in front of me. I looked up and saw two policemen. They demanded my papers. I didn't have any papers. They said they would take me to the station where I would be put in prison. I almost burst out crying. Then two women intervened. They asked to speak to the one of the policeman and took him to one side. I heard the policeman say "a hundred dollars." The women shrieked and argued that they were crazy and I wasn't worth anywhere near that much. I could hear them barter and bargain. They settled on fifty dollars and the police walked away, counting their money.

"'You are a very lucky young man,' one of the gypsy women said to me. 'We have saved you from going to prison.' I didn't know what to say or what to do. They told me to come with them. I followed, a little scared. As we walked off I noticed a couple of men following us. We approached a car parked on a side street nearby and as we got to the car one of the men appeared from behind me rushed forward and opened the back door. I got in, thinking that perhaps I was going to get killed, but somehow knew I wouldn't as then they would never get their money back. As we drove off the woman sitting next to me told me I would have to work for them for a few days until the fifty dollars they had paid the police was paid off. As we drove off I thought of my mother, she probably wouldn't even realize I was missing. That was two years ago."

"But I do have somewhere to go, I have a mother and grandmother and sister. I do have somewhere to go," Maria sobbed. "How long will I have to work for them until I have enough money for my fare home? They promised me I could go home once I have earned enough."

"Oh Maria," Olga said, "You will never go home. They will keep you here as long as you are making them money. You will never be allowed to leave, not ever."

Maria sat shocked as she realized she was trapped and a slave to the gypsies.

"Then I will escape and find my way home on my own," she finally said.

"And how are you going to get home? You have no money, no papers, if you escape there is nowhere to go. You cannot call home and you cannot write either – you are searched every day, sometimes a few times a day. If you do manage to run away, where will you go? Moscow is a big city and if you beg on another pavement in another area you will be in the same situation plus you won't have anywhere to go back to at the end of the day. You will have to live on the streets. Maria, there is nowhere else apart from here. If you work for them and earn good money they are all right. They feed you twice a day, we have this place to stay, it isn't much but it is a roof, and there are many without a roof – that die on the streets as winter sets in. We have each other, there are many with nobody, no one to talk to day after day after day. We are lucky."

Lucky? Maria thought. She knew there and then she would escape, she was not going to spend her life on the streets of Moscow begging for a meal and a roof over her head. There was more to life. She had her ambitions, her dreams, her goals – she was determined that she was not going to lead this sort of life. She would play their game for a while, until the right opportunity and then she would escape and go back to her family, to her village, to her home.

"Now get some sleep Maria, you have been through enough for today. Get some sleep and let's see what tomorrow brings." Olga said, helping Maria over to a corner where a few blankets had been placed on the ground by one of the other women. "Tomorrow things will seem better, and as the days and weeks pass things won't seem so bad after all."

Chapter 6

On the Streets

The next morning at six am the doors to the building were unlocked and the two gypsy women entered, carrying a small bundle of clothing. They told Maria to change. Maria looked around – where could she change? There was no privacy, except the one small smelly room that was both the bathroom and toilet, tiny, with a dirty broken porcelain toilet and a cold water wall tap. There was no hot water, in the winter water was warmed on the stove and everyone would take turns washing from the same big container as their soup and stews were cooked. Maria, maintaining as much privacy as she could, struggled into her new clothes. She guessed these clothes would probably stay on her body for weeks. Clothes were washed, infrequently, in the same large pot.

"And this is for you to get about on." A wooden base with small wheels in each corner was placed on the floor. Maria crawled over and placed herself onto the plinth. The man with one leg took the belt off his worn out old trousers and fed it under the plinth between the wheels and across Maria's waist. He carefully tightened the ancient buckle and she was secured. The gypsies also gave her a pair of old gloves for her hands. She would have to find something better, she thought, as the gloves would soon wear out.

Maria followed the gypsy women outside. The second

woman was waiting, along with three other dirty horrible looking men standing by the car, cigarettes stuck to the corners of their mouths. Two of the men were quite old, around the same age as the women but the third was a lot younger, probably around thirty. His greasy black hair was swept back off face, his dark eyes and dark features betrayed a hard life, an unfeeling and heartless life of poverty and struggle. He looked as though he cared for no one and nothing. He looked down at Maria as she struggled to get used to her new platform, bumping and grinding over the rutted stony ground leading to the waiting car. She got one of the wheels stuck and, as she tried to maneuver herself free, he hooked the end of the shoe under the platform next to the stuck wheel and jolted her free almost causing her to topple over. He laughed as the other beggars looked on, silent, used to the torment and humiliation.

"You had better get used to it pretty quick," he snarled.

The other gypsy men stood and watched as Maria nervously and clumsily made her way to the car. At the door she unlocked the buckle to the belt and Svetlana and Olga helped lift her onto the back seat, placing the platform on Maria's lap. Svetlana sat beside her and Olga walked round the other side, squashing Maria in the middle. One of the older gypsy men got into the driver's seat and the old woman sat in the front passenger seat. As they drove to the Metro, Maria was told she would be working at Kurskaya Metro Station, outside the entrance to the Metro. But first they were to take the Metro to that station as it was too far to drive and they needed the car to pick the others up. Everyone would be working their normal places either at the exit of the Metro or nearby. The gypsy women sternly briefed Maria, telling her that she will be keeping a close eye on her. The important thing was to sit where as many people as possible passed, but not so close that people passed in too much of a hurry or without looking down and seeing her. The gypsies had been working that territory for a few years and knew the local mafia well, but she still needed to introduce the new girl and negotiate a new fee. Maria was warned that she better be worth the extra money the gypsies will have to pay.

It was impossible for her to believe that in a few minutes she would be sitting on the streets of Moscow, so far away from her home and her family, begging to survive. She remembered the few beggars she had seen in her village and thought what a horrible and degrading life it was. She always hurried passed as quickly as she could, or looked down or away. She never gave anything – she didn't feel sorry for them, she didn't feel sad for them, they were just odd people standing silently with their hands out. And now she was going to be part of that strange tormented sad group, and people were going to pass her by, without looking down or even caring. At least, she thought light-heartedly to herself, it was the summer and it was warm. But she would have to escape before the winter.

The car stopped opposite the Metro entrance and they all got out. The driver turned around and went back for the others. Maria buckled herself onto her wooden platform and followed the others as they made their way across the road to the entrance of the Metro. As they approached the concrete steps leading from pavement level down to the Metro entrance, the gypsy woman and Svetlana grabbed Maria each side under the arms and held her as they went down the steps and through the swinging entrance doors.

The gypsy already had Metro tickets for everyone and, keeping a close eye out for police, they went through the turnstile one by one, down the escalator and waited on the platform. Maria had never been on a Metro before but, as they were ushered on and off the train as it came and went, her thoughts were of what was going to happen to her in the next few hours.

At the Kurskaya Metro station, where they were going to spend the following days, weeks, months and quite possibly years begging, Maria was instructed to sit on her wooden platform just outside of the swinging exit doors alongside the wall and hold out her hand, looking up at everyone that passed by. She was told that she was pretty and if she looked pretty people would pity her and give her more. She had to brush her hair and keep her clothes tidy and the gypsies promised that if she did well they might even bring her a little make-up. The gypsies knew a pretty looking girl with no legs begging was sure to generate a lot of money. However, she was firmly told that if anyone asks her what she was doing or where her family was or anything else, she must just say that her family is dead and that she was begging to survive. This would generate even more pity and even more money. Maria felt sick when she was told to say that about her family, and hoped no one would ever ask. The only thing she could say to passers by was "A few roubles please" and "thank you". If she was heard saying anything else she would be punished.

Maria was shown where to sit. It was still early and, although there were already quite a few people going to work, the real rush of commuters hadn't yet started.

She sat, fighting back the tears, hoping that she would soon wake up to find the last few days were just an awful surreal nightmare. Slowly a tear rolled down her eye and onto her cheek, she tried to wipe it away, not wanting the gypsy to see. No matter what she had to go through and how bad things may get, she wanted to be strong, and not to cry.

"You can cry all you like dear," said the gypsy standing over her, looking down, "crying is good for business."

Her eyes filled as she struggled with the words "A few roubles please." As seven o'clock approached the station started getting busier and busier. More and more people made their weary way to work. People passed briskly by, occasionally glancing down at this new sight on their normal mundane journey, perhaps promising to give a few roubles to this poor girl on their way home or maybe tomorrow, or the next day.

Her hands slowly filled with kopecks and roubles and every so often she would wrap the coins she had collected in the cloth placed by her side. And every so often one of the gypsy women would turn up, pick up the cloth, count its contents, pop the money into a leather bag and disappear.

She filled the day with thoughts of her family and her village, her school and her friends, her grandmother's cooking and the books she loved to read. The gypsy women came and went and smiled every time she counted the past couple of hour's takings – nodding or bending over whispering a well done in her ear before scurrying off. Maria felt disgusted and ashamed.

Every morning at six am sharp the door was unlocked and they went to work. After about a week Maria was trusted to make her own way on the Metro to her begging site. But always, within an hour or so the gypsy women would arrive, take the money, counting it, nodding, whispering "well done" and scampering off. She was earning more than any of the others and the gypsies were very happy. As the weeks passed they would occasionally bring her a little make up, or a new blouse. One of the men found an old handle which they attached to a block of wood for Maria to use instead of her old gloves. With the block she could propel herself around on her makeshift platform a lot more quickly and easily. Weeks and months passed. She learnt to manage steps and the escalator, swinging doors and getting on and off the Metro. She would shout at the top of her voice "Beep beep, let me through, let me through," as she darted in and out of the commuters.

And every night she made her way back to the squalid, run down building which was now her "home." The gypsies would always be waiting at the Metro with the car, counting the last money she had collected, searching her and ushering her and the other beggars into the car and back to their hovel. Most of the time the same grubby looking man drove the old Lada, although occasionally the younger man would turn up and drive. He sent shivers down Maria's spine. He smiled at her and tried to make basic conversation but she detested him. There was something about him that was nasty and cruel and horrible and she couldn't bare the thought of him even looking at her.

The two gypsy women were there every morning and every evening but others came and went. Sometimes there were children, rough looking, foul mouthed kids that taunted Maria and the others and ran around the yard, kicking cans, spitting and fighting. Other times old men just stood by, smoking, staring silently as the beggars came and went. Maria wondered who they were and where they lived.

As the summer slowly passed and autumn drew in Maria and the others would often sit outside their dilapidated home, on wooden boxes, eating their soup and bread and chatting after a day on the streets begging, Sometimes they talked about nothing in particular, other times they told their own stories time and time again, as though each time was the first and the perhaps last and somehow their lives would change and this was all a nightmare for them too. They talked about the dreams they once had, the tables they once sat at, the food they once ate. Maria sat and listened – they seemed to be able to talk freely to her. She gave them all a little sparkle of hope as she spoke about going home, of her family and friends, of her escape. They saw something of themselves in Maria – as though they too did indeed have somewhere to go and family waiting for them with open arms and hugs and tears of relief.

In the weeks and months that passed no one else joined their little group, the gypsies had enough beggars working for them. Their group seemed to become stronger and closer, the old ladies helped Maria and Svetlana mend their worn out tatty clothes, the old man serviced Maria's platform, keeping the wheels running smoothly and the block free of splinters.

Everyone understood that Maria was earning good money as they were now getting a few extra "luxuries" that they had never had before. A frying pan was given to them, and once or twice a week sausages were brought to supplement the daily monotony of soup and stew. They would occasionally be treated to white rather than black bread and once a week they were brought fruit.

As time passed she learnt more and more about the gypsy way of life. This group had originally come from an area not far from where she lived. They were a big family, with connections to other gypsy families in and around Moscow. Normally they would not stay too long in one place, as they were usually targeted by the police and, with many gypsies having few or no papers, were quickly moved on after paying heavy fines. But this gypsy family was paying the local police and the local mafia groups and was earning a good living from the beggars. She learnt that the men she would see come and go were the cousins or uncles or perhaps even the husbands of the two gypsy women that had first taken her. They all lived on what the beggars earned every day as well as what they could steal on the streets and from people's homes and cars. She heard that there were various groups of gypsies throughout Russia targeting and kidnapping the old and the disabled, sending them to work on the streets. The "prisoners" would be kept for as long as possible, until they or the gypsies would inevitably be moved on by the police and then they would be sold to another gypsy family in another part of Moscow.

Maria heard stories of gypsy children targeting foreigners in the centre of Moscow. The groups of children would suddenly spring from nowhere, surrounding the foreigners, pulling at their coats and tugging their clothes and distracting and confusing them until their prying searching hands found wallets and passports. Or the gang of children would run past foreigners grabbing at cameras or handbags or jewelry and dispersing in a multitude of directions, down alleys and side streets. Foreigners were easy bait, more and more foreigners were visiting Moscow for holidays and business and they looked so out of place with their western clothes and hairstyles and western look, they were an easy target for the gypsy children.

With her pretty face and big blue sad eyes, Maria was earning good money for the gypsies. People felt pity for her and gave more than they normally gave to other beggars.

Slowly Maria began to make friends with a kiosk worker nearby. She was a fat friendly woman called Lydmilla, who sold newspapers and magazines and greeted Maria every morning and bade her farewell every evening. Lydmilla had been working that specific kiosk for many years she knew of the gypsies and she hated them for what they did. But she kept herself to herself, paying the local mafia every week, ignoring what was going on around her. She knew that if she interfered she would be beaten up and thrown off the territory and it would be very difficult if not impossible to find another kiosk in another area, but Lydmilla had a daughter about Maria's age and felt sorry for Maria. She also knew that the gypsies didn't like their beggars talking much to anyone, and so she would be very careful and only said hello and goodbye whenever she felt sure there was no one nearby watching. She would sometimes leave her kiosk for a few seconds and drop Maria some small change and exchange a few words. As time passed the gypsies began to trust Maria more and more and she would gradually stop for longer and longer at the kiosk. It was never more than a few minutes, but if the gypsies saw her they didn't say anything, even when the kiosk worker openly gave her the occasional women's magazine and puzzle book. This was Maria's plan, to make the gypsies trust her and to show the gypsies that she did indeed have nowhere else to go and that her life was now on the streets. And then, when they least expected it, she would plan her escape.

Chapter 7

The Escape

As time passed Maria noticed a young guy hanging around in the mornings as Maria went out to work and in the evenings when they returned. Sometimes it would just be him with the two women, other times he would be standing smoking with the elders. He kept looking at Maria, smiling and occasionally saying hello and asking how she was and if she was warm enough. The winter was settling in, it was getting colder, snow was falling and life begging on the streets was becoming harder and harder. He started turning up where Maria was begging, bringing her an extra coat or scarf or some new gloves, or some warm tea and frequently stood by her side chatting as she tried to beg. She learned that he was the youngest son of one of the gypsy woman that had originally found her stuck between the railway carriages all those months ago. She didn't like him, he was ugly and his hair was horrible and he was unwashed and smelt dirty but above all he was a gypsy and she detested the gypsies and their way of life with every fiber in her invalid body. She detested the way they treated other human beings, using their disability to their advantage and gain. She hated how they ruled the group with fear and threats of violence and intimidation and how they were all held against their will in that squalid run down cold dirty building. The gypsies were the jailers and they were the prisoners, and she despised them for everything they had done to her and everything they had taken away from her. She tried to ignore him, pleading with him to let her work, but day after day he continued visiting her, spending a few minutes by her side chatting, or bringing her an occasional hot drink, or just standing silently by, watching her. She felt uneasy.

All through the winter he would visit her on the corner where she worked. She was always guarded and very careful with what she would say. She tried not to upset him or to be too rude, as she didn't want to be punished by either him of his family, and was careful never to talk about her family or her desperate desires to return home. She would make a little conversation but, after a few minutes, ask him to move on as she couldn't beg if he was standing next to her. No one would give if they thought she was a gypsy – everyone in Moscow hated the gypsies. His mother also warned him about spending too much time standing with her, but he would ignore his mother's nagging even though he understood he was affecting the amount of money Maria was making. But he liked Maria and it was the only time he could spend with her.

Maria and the rest of her group survived the long, harsh, hard winter. Many on the streets didn't. The cold pierces the heart and numbs the soul and quickly kills many that live and work on the streets. Unless shelter can be found and layers upon layers of warm clothing worn, there is little chance of surviving a Russian winter. Maria and her group were lucky, they had shelter and warm food and enough clothing to ward off the appalling sub-zero temperatures. The daily trudge of winter had passed, the snow had melted, the sun was shining and blossom started to appear on the trees that lined the boulevards. It was a bright spring morning. After a brief chat to Lydmilla at the kiosk and clutching a free copy of last months Cosmopolitan magazine, Maria arrived as usual at her corner and settled into her normal day. She looked up to see the two gypsy women, along with the two elders whom she now knew were their husbands, and the son approaching her. They had seemed a bit strange in the car that morning on the way to dropping them off at the Metro – the man kept looking at Maria through the mirror and the woman kept turning round and smiling, but she thought it was because she had been earning good money again as it was a little warmer and people were not in so much of a hurry to get out of the cold and the snow. In the winter people rushed by – few people had the time to take off their gloves or bury their hands past the layers of clothing for a few roubles. But in the spring and summer they not only had more time and were more likely to stop for a few extra minutes, but it was also so much easier to give – they wore lighter jackets and could get to their change in their pockets or handbags a lot easier than when they wore thick coats and gloves.

The five gypsies stood around Maria and looked down at her. She suddenly felt very frightened. She cowered back and covered her head with her hands, thinking that she was going to get beaten. She had certainly done a few things wrong over the past eight or nine months but, because she was such a good earner the gypsies had turned a blind eye or let her off with a stern warning. She had not yet had the beating the other beggars had warned her about, and now she was desperately tried to think what it was she had done. She looked at her magazine in her trembling hands and cried, "she gave it to me, I didn't buy it, she gave it to me, go and ask her."

The gypsies smiled. "It isn't that dear," Maria was confused, "we have some good news."

"I can go home!" Maria almost shouted.

"Maria, dear, you know this is your home now," the gypsies replied firmly, looking round, making sure no one heard Maria's outburst. "No, we have even better news. You are going to marry our son Zdanko."

It was wonderful news for the gypsies as Maria earned them all a good living but Maria's world tore apart. She felt sick and her eyes filled with tears. She wanted to scream "no" but no sound came out. She just sat there, numb, silent. Zdanko, the disgusting awful son of those monsters. Ugly, stinking Zdanko who she couldn't bare to even talk to, even though he persisted in visiting her almost every day throughout the winter. Maria looked up at the family. No words would come out. She was shocked. She wanted to shout for help, tell everyone passing by whom these people were and what they were doing to her, but she just looked up and smiled. She now knew she had to escape and very soon. The gypsies told her that the wedding would be very soon and she was privileged because many of the local families would be attending. They all wanted to see what a good woman her son was marrying. As they turned to leave, Zdanko hesitated for a few seconds, smiling down at Maria. He wanted to tell her he loved her and that everything would be fine, but he knew she didn't love him, he knew she despised him. But she will, he thought to himself, she will love me eventually.

On the way home that evening Maria stopped for slightly longer than usual with Lydmilla. She had never spoken with her about what had happened but she had to trust someone and Lydmilla was the only person that could help. While pretending to look through a magazine, Maria quickly told Lydmilla how she was kidnapped and smuggled to Moscow and forced to beg as well as what had just happened that morning. Maria begged Lydmilla to help her. She would conceal a few roubles from her earnings every day and pass them to her as and when she could. The gypsies wouldn't notice. Her plan, she told Lydmilla, was to save for the train fare back home and when she had enough she would just disappear. She wondered why she hadn't done it earlier, but was always too frightened of being found out and of being beaten and she was always too unsure of who, or who not to trust.

"Tomorrow morning," Maria quickly whispered, noticing that one of the gypsy women had returned and was walking towards her, "I will give you my mother's address, please write to her telling her I am safe and will be home soon." She folded the magazine and gave it back to Lydmilla as the gypsy approached. Not even looking at Lydmilla the gypsy ushered Maria away, telling her yet again how well she had done begging that day.

Every day Maria started to put aside one or two roubles, dropping them off with Lydmilla as and when she could or on her way home. The gypsies had allowed her to buy the occasional drink and a light snack, but instead of buying two or three drinks she would buy just the one and make it last the whole day and secrete the money she would have spent to Lydmilla. Instead of buying something to eat, she would go hungry and again give the money to Lydmilla.

With no warning she was told the night before that the wedding was going to be the next day. She wouldn't be working that day. She slept little that night, stooped over the filthy toilet bowl vomiting time and time again until there was nothing left inside her. She finally dozed off for a couple of hours before getting up with the rest of her group. The room was silent – no one spoke as they got ready, they ate their bread and drank their tea in strange haunting silence. Maria fought back her tears, her sadness and despair was overpowering and she sat silently as everyone passed her, giving her a quiet hug or kiss or just touching her shoulder. They understood what was going to happen but could do nothing to help apart from offer emotional comfort and support. They were all now good friends and were all deeply sad and distressed. Svetlana held Maria tightly, her arms wrapped around Maria's neck, her warm tears soaking Maria's cheek. "We will always be here for you," she whispered and kissed her.

Maria watched as everyone slowly made their way out of the front door to their usual day on the streets begging, leaving Maria sitting silently, alone in the middle of the empty room that had been her home for almost a year. She looked around at the few small bundles of tatty clothes lying haphazardly on the floor and the crumpled blankets and wooden crates where her friends sat and slept and she suddenly felt lonely and afraid. She had become used to having people around her when she slept, and with her in the morning when she awoke. She had become used to the constant chatter, the occasional laughter and now her home, their home, was as she had never seen it before. Silent and sad.

Once everyone had left, the two gypsy women came back into the room and gave Maria a new white blouse, fresh underwear and new black trousers. She was also handed a small gold chain with a strange looking crest which the gypsies said she could wear for the occasion. They also gave her some make-up and lipstick. They stood by and watched as she changed and then Zdanko's mother pulled over a wooden crate, sat in front of Maria and started to brush her hair. "You look beautiful, my dear, and you will make my son a good wife." Maria stared at her numbly as she concentrated on brushing her hair. "You will be good to him and bear him lots of children." Maria wanted to be sick – she couldn't stand the thought of Zdanko near her let alone anything else. "It will be a fine day and you will behave and do exactly as we tell you, is that clear? This is your home now Maria and everything will be ok. Now don't cry," she said as she saw Maria's eyes filling with water. "Everything will be fine. Zdanko may not be the most handsome of boys but he is a good man and has a kind heart."

They drove to a rundown apartment block about twenty minutes away. It seemed that the whole of the floor was occupied by gypsy families, doors to the separate apartments were wedged wide open and people wondered in and out and up and down the corridors, talking and shouting and swearing to one another. Children were running around, screaming and crying and shouting. The smell of cooking and cigarette smoke filled the air. Maria was ushered down the corridor and into a big room at the very end where a few of the elders sat. As she entered they looked around and greeted her. She didn't really understand what they were saying, she was in a state of bewilderment and shock and couldn't believe in a few hours or maybe minutes she will be married, and married into a family that had kidnapped her and forced her into slavery, forced her to beg and forced her to live in squalor. The thought disgusted her.

Alongside the far wall was a long table filled with food and bottles of wine and vodka. She couldn't remember the last really good meal she had had. In a macabre way she thought that at least she would be able to eat a good meal, and wondered if she could smuggle some food back to her friends, but she didn't feel like eating. If she had legs she would be running as fast as they could carry her and as far away as they would take her. She would run all the way back to Siberia. But she didn't have legs and couldn't run anywhere. She was a prisoner of her own disability.

She looked at the table of food. The gypsies drank wine and vodka and ate ham and cheese and pickles and fish, all bought with the money that she and the group made begging on the streets, as well as from selling the belongings the gypsies stole from the innocent and naïve and mistakenly careless. While she and her friends ate soup and black bread in their squalid hovel, the gypsies feasted like kings.

At the end of the table was an ornate engraved silver cup standing on a higher velvet covered pedestal. Maria wondered what it was for.

"Welcome to our home, you will be part of the family soon and our home is now your home," said one of the elders, drawing hard on a foul smelling cigarette. She didn't understand what he meant. "You will look after Zdanko and make him a good wife, you will give him children and will provide support and money and work hard for him." Was she really hearing this? That she will work hard for him! What does it mean, that he will live off the money she made begging. Is this what being married into a gypsy family means? That she now must beg to support him?

One of the elders stood up, clapped his hands and shouted, calling everyone into the room. Everyone squeezed in, filling every wall and corner. Zdanko was last in and as he entered everyone cheered and applauded.

Maria and Zdanko were ushered to the end of the room where the oldest looking elder stood. He raised his hand and the room immediately fell silent. He greeted and welcomed everybody in a strange dialect that Maria found hard to understand. It was Russian, but it was a Russian that Maria had never heard before. Maria sat silently, numbed, as he read the vows of their marriage. The elder turned directly to Maria and said something to her. She didn't understand and looked to Zdanko. "Say Yes," he whispered in her ear. She didn't want to say yes, she wanted to scream "No," "Never," but she said yes, quietly, almost inaudible. This can't be a legal wedding, she thought to herself as she looked up at the elder standing before her, and to the side at people smiling and nodding. Surely I am not really married? I have not signed anything, or even said anything apart from "yes." The elder picked up the ornate cup and offered it to Zdanko. He said something and sipped the wine inside. The elder then lifted her hand and a small ornate ring was placed on the third finger of her right hand. She looked at the elaborate design of the piece of gold now circling her finger and wanted to tear it off. As the ring slowly slipping into place, her right arm was lifted high in the air and everyone around her cheered and shouted and music blared from a record player.

Everybody danced and clapped to traditional folk songs that Maria had never heard before, the gypsy women scuttled backwards and forwards with plates and glasses, food and wine. People congratulated Zdanko, hugging him, kissing him, patting his shoulders, while ignoring Maria as she sat alone in the corner. She would be a good earner for Zdanko.

Zdanko's mother bent over and whispered into Maria's ear. From now onwards, she said because she was the wife of her son and the son of an elder, a room has been set aside for them both to live. They will live there as man and wife. She must still go out to work every day but now she will be providing solely for her husband, as that is the gypsy way. Sundays she can have off so she can cook and clean and be with her new husband. She longed to return to the squalor of the room she had made her home and the beggars she had made as her friends. She missed them dreadfully.

The celebrations continued late into the evening while Maria sat silently hour after hour, lonely and sad and, for the first time in over a year, wishing she was dead. She feared the end of the evening as she understood what was going to happen to her. They had taken her dignity and her pride, they had forced her into slavery and poverty and the only thing that was left of hers, the only sacred thing would also soon be taken away. She would soon have nothing left.

He forced himself upon her that evening, as she cried and

pleaded for him to stop. As he forced himself into her, tears filled her eyes as she stared up at the blue sky in her head and the fluffy white clouds and the birds and she smelt the lavender and the freshly cut grass and watched as the butterflies darted around playfully.

Night after night her resolve to escape became stronger and stronger. Three weeks after their marriage Maria missed her period. At first she thought she was just a day late, and then two days, and then a week and then, after two weeks, she knew she was pregnant. She now had gypsy blood inside her. At first she didn't tell Zdanko, hoping that perhaps she would miscarriage and the horror of the situation would be quickly flushed down the toilet, but as her belly slowly grew she knew she needed to tell him. He was indifferent, telling her it was expected and it was her duty as a gypsy and as a wife. Zdanko's mother and the other women were ecstatic – being pregnant on the streets would fetch even more money. There was probably not another pretty pregnant girl, with no legs, begging on the streets in all of Moscow and she started to earn a lot more money. Maria knew it and the gypsies knew it and they milked her for as much as they could get, knowing that it would only last a few more months. They made her work from early in the morning until late in the evening, and even during her so called day off. Summer ended and autumn moved in with its wind and rain and cold sleet showers. Maria sat day in and day out on her wooden platform – her hand outstretched scheming and planning her escape. Because she was earning more the gypsies collected from her more often, always praising her, patting her on the shoulder or on the head, telling her how proud they were and what a wonderful wife she made Zdanko. Every day and a few times a day Maria managed to secretly pass a few roubles to Lydmilla and it was soon adding up. If Maria finished before Lydmilla she would stop for a quick chat and, as

A day out in Moscow – an earlier image of Maria visiting Red Square.

A smiling face.

The corner of the dirty metro where Maria still begs to survive.

Getting around – on Moscow's appalling paths and pavements her wooden, wheeled platform is so much easier than a wheelchair.

Back to where it all started – the freight trains that took her to Moscow.

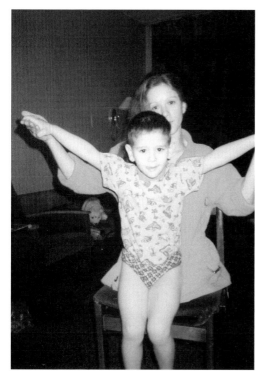

Maria with her son Anton.

Maria in the corridor of the hostel where, from Monday to Friday, she lived alone while her son stayed with Lydmilla.

Maria with Heather Mills-McCartney. When Paul McCartney was in St Petersburg preparing for his concert, Heather flew to Moscow to secretly meet Maria.

Maria, Heather and Inna, with Heather's bodyguard in the background.

At the workshop – where the casts of the sockets are made.

At the workshop and in a good mood.

Creating the sockets – Jamie working on the final measurements.

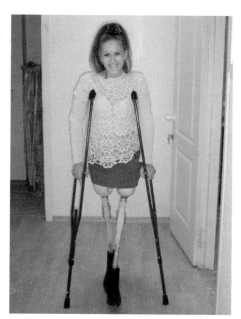

Maria taking her first comfortable steps in over nineteen years.

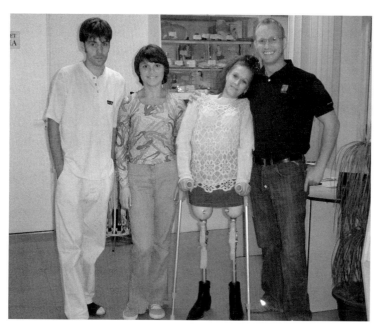

The team that did it – Andrey, Inna, Maria and Jamie.

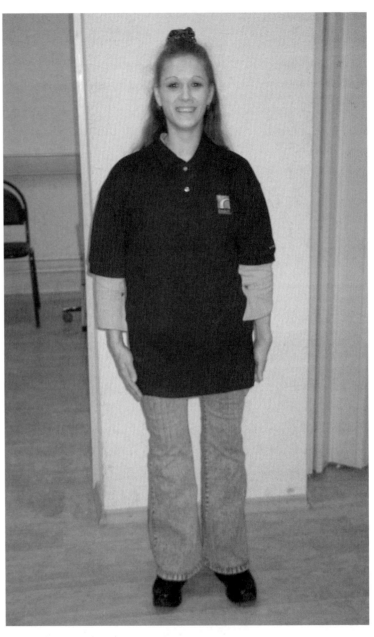

*Maria standing alone – March 2005. Walking for the first
time without any crutches.*

Lydmilla handed her an out-of-date newspaper or magazine she would slip her some change. If Maria had to work
later than Lydmilla, Lydmilla would pass by to say goodbye
when Maria would find a way of slipping her money.

Every day Maria hoped that a reply had come from the
letter Lydmilla had sent her mother. The weeks passed and
there was still no reply. Maria asked Lydmilla to write
another letter, which she did and again weeks went by and
still no reply. Maria wondered if perhaps her family had
moved because maybe her stepfather had finally found
work in another town. Or perhaps the first letter was never
delivered. She knew that posting a letter could take a
month to be delivered, sometimes longer and often they
would go missing and not get delivered at all. The wait for
their reply was the only thing that kept her going. She just
wanted to know that her mother and grandmother were all
right, and that they knew that she was all right and that she
would soon be coming home.

For the following eight months Maria played the game of
a devoted wife and first-rate earner. She never complained,
she tried to always stay strong while all the time planning
and working out her escape. She now had more than
enough money to get back home, she just needed the right
opportunity, for if she was caught she would be punished
and may never have another chance again. That day came
earlier than expected.

One Sunday morning, as Maria was preparing breakfast,
Zdanko casually told her that they would all soon be moving
on, moving to another city. Their time in Moscow was
running out, the police were starting to ask too many questions and demanding higher and higher payments and the
original local police were slowly being replaced by younger,
greedier ones. The street mafia was also demanding higher
payments as the police were extorting more and more from

them too. It simply wasn't worth it so they were planning to move to a smaller town away from Moscow where they would have less to pay and everything would be a lot easier to control. Maria knew she had to act soon, as there would never be another Lydmilla to help her. The following Monday morning, after the gypsies had done their first rounds and she knew she had a little extra time, she spoke at length to Lydmilla and told her of the gypsy's plans. Lydmilla told Maria that everything will be arranged.

Maria hardly slept. She listened to the snores of Zdanko next to her, hoping and preying it would be for the very last time. While she was lying in bed staring up at the ceiling waiting for the clock to strike five she had promised that if everything they had planned failed, if everything collapsed and she was caught or if something stopped her escaping, she would jump into the river and kill herself. It was mid-winter and she knew that she and her baby would die in the extreme cold within a few short minutes. She was determined not to give birth into the horrible world she had found herself. No baby of hers, whether bastard gypsy baby or not, would live the life she had lived and go through the suffering she had gone through. As she felt the baby grow inside her, her feelings slowly changed from hatred and disgust to compassion and acceptance and eventually love. Half of it was hers – her blood and the blood of her family. She grew to love her baby and marveled as it kicked and moved. But she would never let it grow up a gypsy. Never. She would rather die that to let that happen.

She silently got out of bed, brushed her hair, washed her face in the bowl next to the bed and put on her best clothes, hiding them underneath thick layers of jumpers, jackets and coats. She looked around the room, there was nothing she wanted to take. Zdanko stirred and turned over, facing her. Her heart leapt.

"What time is it?" he asked, eyes open, staring at her as she got ready.

"Five thirty," she replied looking at the clock on the wall opposite.

"You're early," he said, sitting up.

"Please don't offer to take me, not today, please no," she screamed inside. He rarely offered, only when the weather was terrible.

"What is the weather like?" he asked laying back down.

She looked through the curtains at the blizzard outside. "It's okay, it's not too bad."

"See you later then," he said and turned over.

"See you later," she replied, wishing with all her heart that she never saw his ugly face again for as long as she lived.

She tightened her buckle over her stumps, threw her small bag over her shoulder and wheeled herself out into the corridor and towards the exit. She could hear others stirring in the rooms behind her, a few calls from some of the children, shouts from the hung-over elders, moans from the women, but she kept on going, wheeling herself as silently as she could down the corridor and away from the gypsies. She unlocked the door and rolled out into the foyer, closing the door quietly behind her. She knew she had to be quick, she didn't have much time. She had to get as far away as possible and as quickly as she could as the gypsies normally made their first rounds about an hour after she left the apartment.

Against the driving snow and bitter cold she wheeled herself as fast as she could towards the Metro. The snow was heavy and quickly built up against her small wheels, bringing her to standstill. She frantically wiped the snow away, always looking over her shoulder for the Lada which would take her to where she didn't want to be. She continued a short distance more, until the snow built up, stopping her again. She pictured Zdanko getting out of bed, seeing the snow and deciding to take her to work after all. Or maybe he would suspect something as he looked out at the blizzard realizing she had lied to him about the weather. She had arranged to meet Lydmilla a few stops further on from her Metro. Lydmilla was already waiting for her on the platform, pacing nervously up and down. Come on Maria, come on, where are you, she said to herself over and over again.

The plan was for them to then catch the Metro together to the other side of Moscow and then take a bus to the farthest outskirts where Lydmilla and her daughter lived. She would stay with them for a while and until she felt safe. They would go together to the country, to a friend of Lydmilla's, where Maria could have her baby.

Maria struggled with the snow until she finally got to the Metro entrance. As Maria got heavier and bigger the platform was a lot more awkward and harder to control. She used to be able to negotiate steps with ease, flying down them sideways using her wooden block as a barrier to her toppling over, but as she got bigger steps became a lot more difficult to negotiate. She was desperate to get to Lydmilla, who she knew was waiting. She managed the first few steps with ease but she was over confident and her weight and awkwardness took hold. She quickly lost balance, spinning and crashing down the steps out of control. Trying hard to stop herself from toppling over completely, she jammed the block into the metal rails that some Metro steps had for prams, jack-knifing onto her side, sliding and bumping her way down the remaining few steps to the bottom. She had slipped out from her buckle and off her platform and lay on her side on the dirty wet floor at the bottom of the steps. Confused and bleeding from a small cut on her forehead, she stared up at the flakes of falling snow on her face. A couple of people rushed over, asking if she was all right. Wet and muddy on one side from the melted dirty snow, she pulled herself upright as someone brought over her platform and her small bag containing her only possessions. As she got onto her platform and tightened her buckle, she heard the squeal of breaks at the top of the stairs and Zdanko's voice cry "Maria, Maria!" Maria's heart leapt.

"Please no," she cried to herself as she frantically wheeled herself passed the kiosks, in and out of the legs of the commuters and into the ticket hall. She already had a ticket and zipped under the baggage opening and onto the escalator, turning round just in time to see Zdanko rush into the Metro. She smiled and waved to him as she disappeared from view – hoping that he would think nothing out of the ordinary and return home rather than continue his chase.

As she got to the bottom of the escalator a train pulled in. She hurriedly wheeled herself onto the platform. As it was the beginning of the line the train was completely empty, but the platform was full and as soon as the doors opened a surge of people pressed forward onto the train, pushing her out of the way and to the back of the crowd. She looked over to the escalators and saw Zdanko jump off the bottom few steps and rush along the platform looking at the passengers and into the carriages. He was getting nearer, surely he could see her? He turned to look directly at her through the crowd. Her heart raced as she pushed herself onto the carriage. Maria watched as he ran towards her. The doors closed. Hearing him smack the departing carriage window with his hands, she was paralyzed with fear as the train pulled away. Maria shuffled and huddled herself in the corner of the carriage, looking up at the sea of bodies hiding her, ignoring her, taking no notice. She felt like vomiting

As the train pulled into her usual Metro station and the doors opened she was almost compelled to leave the train, to go to work as usual, to continue her life of begging for the gypsies. It was a dreadful, undignified, degrading life, but it was a life she knew and she was now frightened of the life she didn't know – of running, of hiding, of always wondering what would happen if they found her. The doors seemed to stay open an eternity, as though they were tempting her, beckoning her. People stood silently waiting for the doors to close and the train to move. She felt they were all waiting for her, as though they all recognised her from the street above, that they had all given her money, and wished her well, and now they were looking down at her questioning as to why she wasn't getting off the train as normal. She strangely felt it was her responsibility to get off the train – she somehow felt she had no right to be anywhere else. Like a clap of thunder breaking her dream the recorded announcement warned that the train was leaving and the doors were closing. As she watched the doors shut she felt that a chapter in her horrible life was also closing and, as the train sped away she felt she was speeding to a new life, a better life, a happier life. For the first time in almost two years she smiled as tears filled her eyes and rolled down her cheek.

Lydmilla paced up and down, looking at her watch and at every train that came and went, scrutinizing the doors as they opened and closed and the passengers as they came and went. "Maria, where are you," she said over and over again. Suddenly from behind her, she heard the screech of Maria's trolley and the frantic thud of the wooden block against the ground. She turned to see Maria's racing towards her, "Quick, quick, he's coming for me," she cried. Logically Maria knew that Zdanko couldn't follow her once she had got onto the train, he would never know when or where she would get off, but the fear of just the possibility of him finding her was greater than the logic that he couldn't. They both turned and raced along the platform and up the escalator.

Lydmilla helped Maria up the stairs, hooking her arm under Maria's left shoulder while Maria used her block to climb the steps, swinging her body strapped tightly to her platform. Although Maria was almost eight months pregnant she wasn't really that big compared to some pregnant women she had seen but, because of her size and her already limited capabilities, it was now virtually impossible for Maria to manage going up steps on her own, she nearly always needed help. At the top of the steps they turned right and rushed through the snow across the square to the bus-stop, Lydmilla ahead slightly grasping Maria's left hand while Maria pushed herself with her block trying to keep up.

"Everything is going to be all right now," Lydmilla said to Maria as they approached the bus stop and joined the queue. "They won't find you now, you are safe," she whispered, as though cautious and suspicious of the others standing around them. She crouched down and wiped the spots of dried blood from Maria's forehead.

The bus arrived and they climbed on. Maria and Lydmilla stood silently staring out through the glass of the rear doors. Maria remembered staring out of the window of the old Lada two years ago when she was first brought to Moscow. Now the snow made everything look clean and new. She watched as people huddled here and there, rushing from the bus to their homes and from their homes to the bus. She remembered the winters in Siberia, her mother or grandmother pushing her wheelchair, hurrying the short distance home from school, always moaning about the weather and the cold, day after day, year after year. She remembered when she had a home to go to, the warmth and smell as she came in from out of the cold. She closed her eyes and remembered her grandmother fussing over her hat, making sure it covered her eyes, and fussing over her scarf, making sure it was wrapped tightly and that her coat was buttoned to the top. As the bus made its way to the very outskirts of Moscow, stopping to let passengers on and off, battling against the blizzard and the pot-holed icy roads and other traffic weaving in and out, she wondered why she had no reply from the letters she had asked Lydmilla to write. Where were they and why hadn't they written? Maybe they *did* move to another village or town.

Lydmilla and Maria got off at the very last stop. Maria looked up and around at all the apartment blocks, like centurions keeping guard on the city, row after row of high-rise concrete blocks, each with their own little front entrance and each entrance leading to the front doors of countless different lives and lifestyles. People came and went – neighbours yet strangers, anonymous lives in an anonymous world.

They made their way fifty or so metres past one apartment block to another. Lydmilla typed the code to the building into the small key pad on the wall and, on the dull sound of a click, opened the heavy front door and struggled into the entrance hall. Lydmilla stamped the snow from her shoes and Maria brushed the snow from her coat and around her platform. They passed the long since abandoned concierge's office to the line of metal post boxes where Lydmilla once again checked her mail, as she had done every single day since posting Maria's letters many months ago. Nothing. She looked down at Maria and shrugged. They made their way up to the twelfth floor in the rickety elevator.

Going into Lydmilla's apartment was the first time she felt that her past was leaving her, that she was now safe and secure and that everything was going to be fine. Smelling the familiar warmth of a home, the sense of serenity and calmness, the feeling of sanctuary was overwhelming for

Maria. She felt confused – lucky to have found this tiny speck of kindness in a harsh horrible world but sad with the thoughts that her friends were still on the streets begging and living in that squalid one-roomed hovel. The past two years seemed a surreal, bizarre dream – she was never married, her husband hadn't raped her time and time again and he wasn't now searching for her, she was never on the streets begging, the gypsies never actually kidnapped her and she never agreed to go to the carriage for a beer with that boy – this was all unreal, a weird surreal fantasy in her mind. She was there with Lydmilla in her apartment in Moscow for other totally different reasons, what had happened never actually happened. And then the baby kicked and moved and she rested her hands on her belly and felt the life that was inside her.

"Hi mum," a young girl's voice called from the living room. Maria looked up.

"This is my daughter Natasha," Lydmilla said. "This is Maria."

"Hi Maria." Natasha bent over and kissed Maria on the cheek. "Mum's told me a lot about you," she said.

"Let's get those muddy clothes off you," said Lydmilla. "Natasha, get Maria some fresh clothes." Natasha spun round and rushed into her bedroom searching through her cupboard and drawers for fresh underwear, jeans and sweater. "And run the bath," she called.

"A hot bath, some good food and clean clothes and you will feel like new," Lydmilla said ushering Maria into the living room.

Maria sat at the small kitchen table in the first clean clothes she had worn in two years. She had had a long bath and felt fresher that she had ever felt. She had just finished her second bowl of the best Borsch soup she had ever tasted and stared out the window at the falling snow she wondered whether her mother and grandmother were doing the same. Were they also staring out of the window thinking about her?

"I remember there was a telephone booth at the post office in my village. Can you help me find the number? I can try to call them. I am sure *they* will know whether my mother and sister have moved." Maria said. Lydmilla nodded.

Natasha was just a couple of years younger than Maria and immediately they developed a close friendship. Natasha helped Maria whenever she could. For the first few days Maria just slept and ate and sat around watching television while Lydmilla went to work and Natasha went to school. Lydmilla came home every evening with tales of the rage and anger of the gypsies. Zdanko had waited at the spot where Maria usually begged for four hours, pacing up and down in the snow, while his mother and the elders searched the vicinity, travelling backwards and forwards from the apartment to the beggars house and back to the Metro. They had questioned Svetlana and Olga and the others, but they knew nothing. They told the local police, who just shrugged, and the local mafia boss, who laughed and demanded that they continue to pay for Maria's place anyway. This enraged the gypsies even further. Zdanko searched their room, ripping up and destroying everything that belonged to Maria. Maria smiled at the stories but still felt a sense of fear that one day they will catch up with her and make her pay and a deep sense of sadness that her friends were still on the streets.

They had arranged for Maria to stay with some of Lydmilla's relatives at a small town about thirty kilometres from Moscow. Maria would stay with them until she gave birth. The day before they left Maria was given an appointment at the local hospital to have a scan. She hardly slept the night before, tossing and turning. When she wanted to sleep her baby kept her awake, kicking and moving – somehow sensing that later that day Maria would see it for the very first time. On the streets Maria wasn't given any opportunity to visit the hospital and so, after Lydmilla had briefly explained the situation to the doctors, they urged Maria to visit them as soon as she could. They couldn't actually believe that Maria had been working on the streets for so long, in the condition she was in, with her disability and without any kind of pre-natal care whatsoever.

The blizzard had passed, the sky was clear and the snow sparkled in the sun. Their breath lingered in the air as they slowly walked the few blocks to the hospital, Natasha and Lydmilla either side of Maria as she wheeled her way over the hard icy pavement. Maria was uneasy. She would soon see the result of what had happened to her – the product of the false arranged gypsy marriage, the product of her forceful, uncaring husband. She had grown to love the child inside her, it had become part of her as she had become part of it, and now, for the first time, she would see this wonderful being and understand what and who it really was and that they were inexorably linked. Her past was no longer just her past but her past was now her future. What was growing inside her would be with her and part of her forever, until she was old and grey and after she was gone from this world. The child would grow and have children of its own and they would have children of their own and the past could and would never ever be just the past but always part of the future. And anyway, she wondered, was it a girl or a boy?

It took almost a week for Lydmilla to find the number of the post office in the centre of Maria's village. She had to make lots of calls from the payphones in the Metro and numerous trips to Moscow's central post office but the day before they were due to go to the hospital Lydmilla had finally got the number and had called and spoken to the director of the post office himself. The family had not moved but there was talk of news, bad news that had happened a while ago. He was not sure exactly when. They had all heard about Maria's disappearance, the despair of the family, one tragedy after another, poor souls. The grandmother had passed away shortly after Maria had vanished, the stress was just too much, but there was more bad news that should and could only be told to Maria herself. Even though Maria had plagued Lydmilla every day for news she had decided not to tell her until after she had visited the hospital. As they walked silently together, Maria with her thoughts about the child inside her and Lydmilla wondering what other tragedy will soon befall this poor young girl.

Maria stared at the image of the baby filling the screen in front of her. It was a boy, a beautiful baby boy. She cried as she watched mesmerized as he moved and at his tiny heart beating life inside her. Lydmilla and Natasha stood either side of the bed holding Maria's hand, captivated by the screen.

"You have a healthy baby boy, as far as we can tell there is nothing wrong with him, he looks beautiful," the doctor said.

"He is beautiful," Maria replied, looking up at Lydmilla.

"Now you must rest, take it easy. We will get you a wheelchair to get around on, it might be a bit easier and certainly a lot safer than that thing," he said, pointing to her platform propped up against the wall in the corner.

"I understand you are going to the country for a while?" he asked Lydmilla, who nodded.

"I would prefer that you stay here so I can keep an eye on you, everything looks fine but... with your disability," he said to Maria, "it is better that we keep a close eye on you. Think about it."

Lydmilla and Natasha helped Maria off the bed and onto

her familiar platform. She strapped and buckled herself on and, following the doctor and Natasha, wheeled herself out of the clinic and down the corridor. At the end of the corridor the doctor turned to go into his office as Maria promised to return in a couple of days to pick up her wheelchair. She wouldn't, she didn't want a wheelchair, she was quite happy with her wooden platform – she could go almost anywhere on it but in a wheelchair she would go nowhere. She also didn't want to go back to see the doctor, she was looking forward to seeing the country again and wanted to get away from Moscow. She would have her baby in a place where the air was cleaner and where it was quieter and calmer.

At the junction of the path to the apartment and the Metro, Lydmilla told Natasha to take Maria back home as she wanted to make a few more telephone calls, just in case there was news on the telephone number to the village. Maria insisted that she go with her but it was now the afternoon, Lydmilla said, and even if she did get the number there would not be anyone at the post office in Eastern Siberia at that time of the day – they were two hours ahead of Moscow but she promised that if she did manage to get the number she could call tomorrow as her relative has a telephone at her apartment.

Holding hands, Maria and Natasha wondered back to the apartment laughing and giggling and chatting about the baby and how amazing it was to see it on the television screen. Maria was nineteen years old, she would be twenty just a few days after her baby was due to be born. As they walked towards the apartment Maria looked up at Natasha who, at seventeen, was the same age she was when she was almost raped in the carriage and kidnapped. As she looked at Natasha, her innocence and naivety, she wondered how she had ever survived the previous two years.

It was almost a new century. What would this next year bring, Maria thought. For the last two years she had lived in misery, would this new millennium bring something better, a life with a beautiful baby, a new life? Her adolescence had been taken from her, the purity of youth and the innocent experience of discovery, but what would she do now? She wanted to go home, to her mother and grandmother, to her sister and her little apartment. She wanted to curl up on her bed and smell the fresh linen and pick flowers in the summer and cook soup for everyone in the winter and get back to a normal life, a life with a new beginning, with a wonderful, beautiful son whom she could adore and spoil and play with and love – just as her mother had done with her when she was little.

"Maria, Maria – I have the number," Lydmilla screamed rushing through the front door. "I have the number of the post office and I called them myself, I did! There *was* someone still there, I spoke to the Director of the post office himself and he told me he would go to your parent's apartment tonight and tell them the good news and tomorrow you can speak to them yourself! You can call them midday tomorrow!"

They had woken very early that morning and took the first train to the village where Lydmilla's relatives, Sasha and Irina, were waiting on the platform. Lydmilla had already explained everything to them and as the clock neared twelve noon, they all silently left the room. All morning Maria had thought about what she was going to say, how she was going to explain everything. There were so many things she wanted to tell them. She looked down at the bulge of her belly and smiled as she thought of telling her mother that she was going to be a grandmother. That would be the very first thing, before anything else. She would tell her what a beautiful, wonderful grandson she will have. Her mother will be so happy. Maria closed her eyes and imagined her excitement, of her mother and her sister and her grandmother jumping around, clapping, laughing, smiling, and urging her to come back to them and their home and the village as soon as she could. She could hear them say that everything was now going to be all right and that they would all look after little Maria and her son as they had looked after her before she disappeared. She smiled to herself as she thought of their warm arms around her, hugging her tight, their tears of joy, their excitement, their friendship but most of all their love. She had so missed their love.

Maria sat trembling with her fingers over the telephone. She dialed the number and waited, silence. No connection. She tried again, silence, and again, no connection. She looked up at the clock, five past twelve. She tried for the third time, and then the fourth, still no connection. Twelve fifteen. She tried once more and, after a few seconds, there was the familiar sound of the phone ringing. Maria's heart leapt.

"Hello?" Maria said timidly, shaking with nerves.

"Hello Maria!" screamed a voice Maria didn't recognize on the other end, "Maria, is it you? Is it really you? Oh my god Maria, We thought you were dead, Oh Maria where have you been?" she heard crying.

"Oh Nadezhda, it's you!" Maria screamed back "My little Nadezhda." Maria heard her sister weeping hysterically on the phone, "its okay Nadezhda I am all right now, everything is all right, don't cry my little Nadezhda don't cry" Maria said over and over. "Where's Mummy, let me speak to Mummy," she asked

There was a silence apart from her sister's sobs.

"Oh Maria, Maria, Mummy's dead, Nikoly came home one night really drunk," she sobbed, "he tried to hit me,

Mummy stepped in the way and he hit her. She fell and hit her head, Oh Maria, Maria, Mummy's dead."

Maria sat silent, stunned, unable to talk or move.

"And grandma?" Maria whispered

"Grandma died a few weeks after you had gone missing. She died of a broken heart Maria." All her hopes of going back to her family were shattered. Her dreams that had given her the strength during the past two years to fight her situation and had driven her to escape the gypsies and the suffering and the squalor and the deprivation of her life had vanished. A deep black hole had opened in front of Maria – the world spun around her, images of her life on the streets mercilessly tormented her, ruthlessly taunting her. She looked down into the gaping black hole beneath her, into the world darkness and of nothing and fell in, willingly.

Maria collapsed.

For almost two weeks Maria laid curled up in bed, eating little, saying nothing. She didn't cry, there were no more tears left, there was nothing left just an empty space; no thoughts, no feelings, just an empty space in her mind as she stared down into the swirling hole. The hole was safe, nothing more could hurt her, nothing more could happen to her and she never wanted to leave it. She wanted to die.

Sasha and Irina looked after her, talking to her, urging her to get up, to eat something, to watch the television or read or just to do something. She didn't want to do anything. She didn't want to live. There was no reason to live, she had nothing to live for and she had no one. Her youth had been taken from her, her innocence and purity, her normality – everyone that she ever loved had also been taken. What had she done to deserve the life that she had been given? If she had only sat still on the train all those years ago when they were on their way to see her grandmother nothing like this would have happened. She would not have fallen from the train, she would not be disabled, she would not have been kidnapped, she would not have had to beg, she would not have been raped and, above all, her mother and grandmother would still be alive. Was she to suffer eternally because of her inquisitiveness when she was just five years old? Was she being punished, were those around her being punished because of the actions of an innocent little girl? Was she solely responsible for everything that has happened to her and around her – is there not one good thing in this life to compensate for everything bad and ugly and horrid?

And then the baby inside her kicked. She opened her eyes. It kicked again and again. She propped herself upright. He was telling her not to give up, that he *was* the one good thing in her life that had made the pain and anguish of her life worthwhile. He was not going to let his mother go. He needed her and he was ready. "Irina," she called. "Irina!"

On the 26th January 2000 Maria gave birth to a beautiful baby boy. She named him Anton It was the name her mother would have chosen had she had a son. Lydmilla was his godmother.

PART THREE

Walking Tall

Chapter 8

Back to the UK

Tears rolled down Inna's eyes as the clouds rolled in and we rushed into a dark corner of the dirty Metro to shelter from the heavy rain. The rain battered against the grimy window behind the row of kiosks where we had settled, there was no place else and the station was packed with people waiting at the exit until the rain subsided.

I stood in front of Inna and Maria as they sat huddled against the grubby wall. I listened to Maria talking in Russian to Inna, not knowing what was being said but by just looking at the expressions on Inna's face I knew that the story was sad and tragic but astonishing. Maria told Inna that she spent about a month with Sasha and Irina looking after the baby. Lydmilla and Natasha visited them every weekend. She was so proud of little Anton, every hardship, every trauma, every difficulty was worth just one minute holding Anton in her arms, his face close to hers, his wonderful smell. He was the most beautiful thing she had ever seen. She was going to be a good mother.

Lydmilla heard that the Gypsies had moved on, no one knew where, but apparently they were no longer in Moscow. Maria wondered about her friends the beggars, what had become of them? Where were they now? Had they gone with the gypsies or sold to another clan? Were they still on the streets somewhere? Did their dreams come

149

true? She thought about them often but had not seen them since.

Lydmilla, with Sasha's help, managed to find Maria one room at a hostel in Moscow. It wasn't much but it was a place of their own. It cost just a few roubles a night.

After a month in the country with Sasha and Irina, Maria and Anton went back to Lydmilla's apartment for a short while until they moved into their room. Maria was no longer alone. She had friends, good kind friends and she had Anton – she is loved and she could now love.

Lydmilla and Natasha look after Anton from Monday to Friday, while she still begs from morning until night. She has little choice. She must pay the local mafia boss, but he isn't greedy and leaves her alone. She said she found this spot about three years ago, has lots of friends in the area and has remained here ever since. She earns just enough to support herself and Anton. She stays alone at the hostel during the week and at weekends either Natasha brings Anton into Moscow or Maria goes to stay with them. Anton is a bright little boy and he goes to kindergarten, which he loves.

Maria eventually went back to Siberia, but things were different and awkward and she didn't stay long. Her sister lived in their mother's apartment, but after a tearful reunion and a couple of days of somber hanging around, she left. There was no longer anything for her in her village and she no longer felt close to her sister. Her life was in Moscow with her son.

Inna looked up at me, wondering what to do or to say. "What a story," she finally managed to utter, looking down at her notes.

I asked Inna to explain to Maria that we shall try and sell her story to a British newspaper or magazine and that she has our word that we would give her any money we make from selling it. Inna translated.

"We will see." Maria said, "To be honest, a lot of people tell me they will try and help, but nobody ever does. Thank you anyway, but let's see."

"It may take a while but I promise you that we will try our best." I replied. I really didn't want to be one of those whose promises vanished with the change of season, I felt determined. I wanted to at least try and do something for her and writing a story and selling it to a newspaper or magazine seemed the only way.

"And anyway, I'm not going anywhere." She laughed.

Inna took out an envelope we had already filled with a few hundred roubles and handed it to Maria, saying it was for her time. I shook her hand and kissed her cheek and thanked her in my limited Russian. As we said our goodbyes neither Inna nor I wanted to leave. We had a strange feeling of guilt and of responsibility. We felt that Maria and Anton should be leading a different life, not the life they have had and have now, but a "normal" life, a life like most other mothers and children around the world. As we walked away, looking back, waving, smiling, we felt sadness and despair for her, her son and her life. Life on the streets of Moscow was now the only life she knew, but she didn't deserve to have been dealt the hand she had, she wasn't a nasty, unkind woman, she wasn't evil, she wasn't uncaring. Sure, she was a tough woman, a strong woman, a bloody minded woman – she has had to be – but she has compassion and kindness and gentleness hard to imagine from a woman that has led, and still leads the life she does. As we walked towards the café and the warmth of our very different world we took one last look back and saw she had settled herself back into her little corner. The rain had stopped and the streets were muddy and we watched Maria, hand outstretched, asking passers by for a few roubles.

As we sat going over Inna's notes in the café, sipping cappuccino, occasionally looking out onto the streets and in the vicinity of the Metro, we wondered what would eventually become of Maria and her son. Inna was summarising the story to me, highlighting a few things, skipping others. She would type it up fully later that evening when we got back to the sanctuary of our apartment and, as I listened to her, I wondered how many others like Maria have a story to tell. I remembered the man with no arms on the Metro standing in front of me many months ago on that very first day I saw Maria, and wondered again about his story and the life he now leads.

Weeks passed and I had finally managed to put a draft story together from Inna's six pages of notes and hours of "filling in." We had spoken about Maria and Anton many times over the previous weeks but I had been busy finishing a few other stories. I also had a five-day close protection operation. I had been tasked to provide security for two corporate clients who were regular visitors to Moscow. It was an easy job, but took up my time and energy and it had postponed finishing the article on Maria. I suppose I had fallen into the trap of what I didn't see I didn't think about, although that wasn't entirely true, but I had put back her article and trying to sell it until I had more time, and, after almost a month, it was finally finished and ready to sell. I also had a couple of nice pictures of Maria to go with the article.

When trying to sell a story freelance to magazines and newspapers it is always best to first send a synopsis, rather than the finished article. Editors get hundreds of different unsolicited articles and editorials every week from freelancers like me, almost all go into the bin and so the first few seconds are the most important. I had to grab the editor's immediate attention otherwise the e-mail or fax would simply be ignored. Editors rarely reply, so you don't actually know whether they are considering your story or whether it ends up in the trash can. I sent a synopsis of

Maria's Story to about twenty magazines, mainly woman's weeklies, as well as a couple of more mainstream monthlies. After about two weeks of sending e-mails and faxes and chasing them up I eventually heard back from around four – all saying what a tragic story it was but it wasn't really for the British market. If it featured a British girl then they would definitely be interested, but not a Russian girl. As the replies slowly filtered into my inbox we became more and more despondent, we had promised Maria we would help and the only way we felt we could was by selling the story and giving her the proceeds, but we couldn't sell the story. We didn't know what to do and we didn't know what we would tell Maria if and when we saw her again. Inna had told me that there were times that she saw Maria on the streets begging but had to take a different route into the Metro as she felt embarrassed about not having done anything. It would have been easier for us to have ignored her, to put her tale and her circumstances down to one of life's many sad tragedies and continue with our own lives, hoping we would never see her again. That would have been far easier but we felt guilty and obligated and we promised ourselves we didn't want to be like all the others – saying they will definitely do something but actually ending up doing nothing. We had given Maria our word that we were going to help her, and that was what we decided we were going to do.

Moscow is sometimes the most wonderful place to live; vibrant, exciting, energetic, unique, but it can also be a dreadful place – high crime, extreme corruption, violent, immoral. Sometimes you love the city and everything about the city and everything that living in Moscow means, but other times you crave to escape to the normality of the west, to the security and stability, to the relative honesty and incorruptibility of a more modern society. I had had enough of Moscow and the breaking point came when, one day, Inna and I sat in the kitchen drinking tea, reading, and occasionally looking out onto the magnificence of the Moscow State University. It was a nice day, we had the windows open, the music playing and were enjoying the breeze and the fresh smell from the park nearby. There was little traffic along the narrow road in front of the apartment, only the occasional car pulling into the car park in front of the building or on its way to the neighbouring block, and we could hear the light hearted chatter of the concierge below. We got on well with Alex. He lived in the apartment directly opposite and had helped us out on several occasions – and had even once got us back into our apartment when the door lock broke during the first few days of us moving in. He had been working as the concierge for a few months after persuading the rest of the residents that he could and would do a better job that the existing concierge, who did little all day apart from sitting cooped up in his dingy office getting drunk. Alex organised games for the children and quiz evenings and even had floodlights installed after one of the residents was attacked outside the block the previous winter. When the rubbish in the shute become blocked, it used to stay that way for days, stinking and rotting in the heat of the summer as the refuse from the apartments above piled higher and higher, but Alex would call the engineers and have it unblocked and fixed almost immediately. When the ice outside the entrance would build up and become almost impassable and treacherous, he would be up at six am with his shovel clearing the snow from the paths. He got paid almost nothing, but loved his job and spent every minute of every day working for the community and helping out where and when he could. Around fifty years old, white hair, always smiling and friendly, Alex wasn't a frail man, but he wasn't particularly fit and healthy either.

Suddenly we heard shouting and commotion outside and looked out of the window to the ground below. Alex seemed to be having a heated argument with a young policeman who had just left the building opposite. He was flapping some papers around, shouting and swearing about something. Inna was trying to listen. The policeman started shouting back, which seemed to make Alex even angrier and argue even more. Suddenly the policeman rushed over and grabbed Alex by the arm, forcing it behind his back. We heard Alex cry for help. I rushed to get my camera – I wanted to photograph this as, in my opinion and not understanding what had been said, Alex didn't deserve this sudden hostility and aggression.

A police car pulled up, probably originally to pick up the policeman. Noticing the commotion another officer jumped out of the car and rushed over to his colleague. They kneed Alex in the stomach, hit him hard round the head and punched him in the face. Alex fell to the ground and they dragged him over to the police car and violently forced him into the back. He was shouting and calling for help but no one listened or helped, they just quickly walked by, ignoring what was going on, frightened of saying anything or of getting involved. No one trusted the police and most people were frightened of them. In Russia the police can still more or less do what they wanted – they were all corrupt, there was no accountability and they would all stick together. I wanted to take some photographs but Inna stopped me. If they knew I had taken photographs or saw the flash they would have certainly stormed the apartment, confiscated the camera and the film, arrested me and taken me to the police station where I would have probably been beaten and held for god knows how long. Russia, one of the biggest and wealthiest countries in the world has one of the worst police forces and, being a foreigner, I had few rights. The police care for no one and nothing and certainly not an old white haired man standing up for himself and whatever he believed in. His wife had heard what was going on and rushed down to help but she too was forced into the back of the police car and driven off. Neither of them came home for three days, when they did they were quiet and withdrawn. Alex told us that, because he swore and insulted a policeman, they had beaten him up and kept him without food or water. I always knew that Moscow was a difficult place to live, a place where its leader was supposedly democratically elected but where there was, in fact, very little democracy.

I hated myself for standing by, watching, unable to do a thing while a friend of ours got beaten up and arrested. It would have never happened in England. Although England has many faults, it is based and built upon an individual's freedom and human rights but in Russia individual rights are ignored and disregarded and it sickened me. I realised there and then that I no longer wanted to live in Russia – I knew that I could no longer live in a country where its people were simply ignored.

This was the last straw after another incident a couple of months previously. I had taken about a hundred manuscripts to the post office where they were to be posted to publishers and magazines around the world. Because of the quantity the clerk agreed that she would weigh them and calculate the postage, assuring us that she would put the stamps on and post them when she had more time. We gave her the money – about one hundred and fifty dollars. Weeks and weeks passed and, after receiving not one reply, we realised that something was wrong. She hadn't posted the manuscripts after all, probably pocketing the money and binning the envelopes. We had always had lots of trouble with our post – letters were always being opened, things stolen, personal mail went missing. So, with the missing manuscripts, the situation outside with Alex and along with everything else I had come to hate about Moscow, Inna quit her job with the security company and, on the 12th October 2003, we moved back to the UK – back to normality and relative stability.

Prior to moving to Moscow I had lived in Manchester. Although my daughter still lived there I didn't really want to go back – I didn't like the city and it seemed too much like Moscow. I had had enough of a big city life and yearned for somewhere more quiet and relaxed, and so we chose to move to Norwich, the city in which I grew up.

I wasn't born in Norwich, but moved there when I was about five, after my father had an affair and had deserted us for the high life in Australia. Before moving to Norwich me, my younger brother and my mother lived in poverty in a caravan in Langley, near Slough. My mother moved to Norwich as her mother and father, as well as two of her brothers, lived there and it would be easier for my mother to be closer to them.

My grandfather was a decorated Second World War fighter pilot and had been based at RAF Coltishall. He was Polish and my mother was born in Poland but moved to England just after the war. I grew up and went to school in Norwich so it seemed the most appropriate place to move back to.

Norwich is a nice city, it has a beautiful Cathedral, an imposing castle overlooking the centre of the city, lots of cafes and bars, a vibrant nightlife, cinemas, theatres and enough culture for Inna and I to feel happy and settled. With a population of about a hundred and fifty thousand it was a far cry from the twelve million or so said to be living in Moscow. Arriving in Norwich from Moscow was like entering a completely different world. The pace of life was so slow and relaxed and, at first, it drove us both mad. We would be hurrying around like idiots while everyone else meandered along without a care in the world. We would rush madly to wherever we were going, racing across the roads, zipping in and out of everyone only to find those we were meeting late, or the meeting cancelled. We would stand in the queue getting more and more frustrated as the shop assistant engaged in a cheerful conversation about something trivial like the weather, or aunt Mavis's new shoes, oblivious to the line of people waiting. And amazingly the people waiting in the queue didn't seem to care either, they were busy chatting to themselves. It was only Inna and me getting more and more irritated and irate.

It took us quite a few weeks of settling into the Norfolk way of ambling aimlessly through the streets, or driving as though there was no other vehicles on the road, or chatting about frivolous things to cashiers and sales people, or taking forever to chose the right margarine, or stopping suddenly in the street for no apparent reason or talking and texting on the mobile in the middle of the road when the lights are green. Unlike Moscow, nobody seemed that bothered in Norwich.

It took Inna even longer to understand the Norfolk accent. Probably one of the laziest accents in England, Inna just could not comprehend what the majority of the people in Norwich were talking about, even though she had studied English at university and spoke it almost fluently. They would greet her in the shop with "Hi-ya-aw-rite" which meant "Are you all right." Missing the first letters of most words and joining two or three words together frequently made the people in Norwich very difficult to understand and Inna took a few months to really adapt herself to this new, strange form of the English language.

Norwich had changed considerably since I left the city about twelve years previously and we both felt it was definitely going to be a nice place to settle. There was the new Forum and library, the new Castle Mall Shopping Centre and another shopping mall under construction, loads of cafés and restaurants, two or three big screen cinemas and the new Riverside complex. However, there was one bad thing about Norwich that I noticed on our first evening out. It was the life on the streets after about midnight. Although, when I was a lot younger, I had worked at many of the nightclubs in Norwich, I never remembered the city centre being so aggressive and polluted with drunks and stupidity and fights and general disregard for others and the environment as it seemed now. Sadly, according to all the media reports, this was not just a Norwich problem but a problem nationwide. As Inna and I walked up Prince of Wales road at around midnight I was appalled at the behavior of everyone around me and embarrassed and ashamed at being English. Inna had never experienced anything like that in her life. Drunken girls were throwing up in the gutter or lying unconscious in alleyways or by the side of the road. Groups of men were fighting, people were shouting abuse at each other and at no one in particular, spitting, falling over while groups of police just stood around watching it all.

"Is this how English people behave?" Inna asked in disbelief.

"Awful, isn't it?" I replied disgusted.

I was taking my Russian wife out into Norwich for the very first time and I was embarrassed and shocked at the behavior of its people. To most foreigners we must seem like utter barbarians and complete animals. If anyone behaved in this way on the streets in Moscow they would be beaten by the police and put in prison.

"If this is what living in a free society does to people, maybe we should go back to Russia," Inna said and I agreed. Moscow is frequently suppressive and often cruel and unkind, but the streets are clean, there is no obvious drunkenness, fighting is dealt with swiftly and sternly and never, ever would a Russian girl be seen intoxicated. Sure, all Russians drink but you would never ever see a Russian girl with her arse in the air vomiting into some gutter while her friends whooped and wailed around her. Inna simply could not understand it. After that first night out we have never been into Norwich that late again, nor do we ever want to. Norwich is great apart from three or four nights of the week after the pubs close.

Inna and I both felt guilty at not having done anything for Maria. We were coming back to England because we couldn't stand living in Moscow, life there was simply too hard and things didn't go as we had planned. We were affected by corruption and crime and yet Maria sat day after day at her place outside the Metro with her hand outstretched asking passers-by for a few roubles. Every Monday morning she would wrap herself up, layer upon layer against the biting relentless bitter winter, leave her son with her Lydmilla and Natasha and travel to her oneroomed dingy apartment at the hostel nearer to the centre of town where she would stay until Friday. She would get up every morning at six and go to bed alone every night, wishing the week would pass quickly so she could be back with her son, playing and laughing and being a mother and friend. We moaned about a few problems and difficulties we had when Maria lived a life we could never live, she endured conditions we simply would not survive in.

As the evening drew in we sat in the back garden of our little apartment drinking cheap red wine and shivering a little with the autumn breeze discussing Maria and what could we possibly do to help her. We could not afford to financially support her ourselves – things were going to be difficult enough anyway during the forthcoming few months. I would have to find paid work as living in England was going to be hugely more expensive than living in Moscow and Inna couldn't work. Where I used to be able to get by on two or three hundred pounds a month, earning that a week in England would still not be enough to pay all the bills. Inna only had a six month visa with no facility to work, so I would have to support her. We had no possessions and no furniture, we quite literally returned from Moscow with two bags full of clothes. Our apartment was decorated with what meager things we had managed to borrow from a few friends. Despite our poverty and hardship we still desperately wanted to do something for Maria, we wanted to honor our promise to her. After lengthy discussions and more cheap red wine, we decided to start a small appeal and try and collect some money which we would then give to her when we next met. I persuaded Inna that people in Great Britain were actually quite generous when it came to charity and giving. We had lots of different kinds of charities catering for lots of different needs and conditions and I felt sure that, with a lot of hard work, dedication and absolute honesty we could collect at least a few hundred pounds. Inna didn't believe me as no one did anything much for anyone in Russia. She simply couldn't believe we literally had thousands of charitable organizations, all trying to do something good for the community, or the disabled, or the poor or the unfortunate. From the huge international charities like the Red Cross to the tiny one-man-band, Britain and the British can be so generous and kindhearted and so moved to give. Inna asked how people could give when things cost so much in England, how could people care for others when it took so much will power and strength just to care for themselves? She was dumbstruck when I told her that the twenty or so dollars we paid every month for all the utilities in Moscow would not last more than a couple of days in the UK. We had rent, electricity, gas, water, council tax, house insurance, television hire, television license, telephone, car insurance, road tax, MOT, personal insurance, mobile phone – the list goes on and on. I told her that to live comfortably most households had to have two very good incomes.

What about children, she would ask. What happens when a couple wants children? I explained either they get thrown into poverty, struggling to survive on just the one salary, or the child quickly goes into daycare and the mother rushes back to work. This was also incomprehensible to Inna. Why would a society charge so much that it forces families either into poverty or to break apart. I found it almost impossible to answer. I found it impossible to answer the many questions she asked about life in England and she simply did not believe me as I tried to persuade her that we could and would raise money for Maria. She thought it was impossible in a society that she initially saw as being incredibly greedy, incomprehensibly expensive and extremely aggressive.

Chapter 9

Heather Mills-McCartney

The next day I designed some leaflets which we had printed. On the front of the leaflet was a picture of Maria sitting on her wooden platform and on the back a brief description of her and her life and an appeal for help. We gave our home address, our home and mobile telephone numbers and an e-mail address, as well as inviting anyone to come and see us at anytime to discuss Maria and her story in greater detail. We also had a few more photos ready to show any visitors we might have. Although we were not a registered charity – just two individuals with a strong desire to help someone over two thousand miles away and in a country most people knew or cared little about – we wanted to show that we were absolutely genuine and we were determined to be as open, honest and transparent as we could.

We bought a street plan of Norwich and plotted a route around the local area. At that time we lived at the very end of a small close, near the Hewitt School and about twenty minutes walk from the city centre. It was a nice quiet middle class area, with rows of neat semi-detached homes with clean and tidy cared-for gardens and company cars parked in neat driveways. We ambitiously had ten thousand leaflets printed which cost us almost two hundred pounds. Inna worried but I assured her we would make the money back and, hopefully, a few hundred pounds extra.

One Sunday morning about two or three weeks after Christmas 2003, and once the leaflets had been printed and delivered, we got up fairly early, put on our comfortable boots and light jacket, as it didn't looked like rain, and headed for our first bout of leafleting the local neighborhood. We spent about an hour and a half popping leaflets through people's letterboxes, until dark ominous clouds moved overhead and the rain started. As the heavens opened up we both huddled under a tree getting wet through. We laughed to each other as we got wetter and wetter, wondering what Maria would have thought if she could see us now, getting soaked trying to raise money for her. I don't think she would have thought "how nice" but probably "how stupid" and she would have almost certainly thought we were both out of our tiny minds. Nobody sitting on the streets of Moscow thousands of miles away would believe what we were trying to do, or why. It would have been incomprehensible to almost everyone. But we had promised Maria, and we were determined to fulfill our promise.

Once the rain had eased off we rushed home, showered and sat next to the radiator with a hot mug of tea trying to warm up while looking out of the window as the sun came out and the weather changed back to a nice sunny afternoon. God must have thought how stupid we were too.

I don't know what I expected but every morning for the following two or three days I rushed to greet the postman, hoping for something, however small. And then on Thursday a cheque for five pounds fell on the doormat. It was our very first cheque, from Mrs. Hingley, with no address, just a cheque and the leaflet. We were delighted. It was only five pounds but it was a start, a glorious start to a long road ahead. I stood admiring the cheque and reciting the proverb about oak trees and acorns. Inna just thought I was mad but every Sunday for the following few weeks we religiously went out with our box of leaflets, walking up and down driveways and paths, getting our fingers trapped in letterboxes, barked at by dogs and occasionally snarled at by suspicious householders. Ever so slowly we started to collect money, five pounds here and there and an occasional cheque for ten, fifteen and sometimes even twenty pounds. We listed every donation – the amount, from whom and the address when given. Suddenly, on the 16th February a cheque landed on our door from J Ogden for a hundred pounds. We couldn't believe our eyes and then on the 19th February David and Barbara Herman sent us two hundred and fifty pounds and the Tuesday before Inna was due to fly her Russian group, whom she teaches Russian to once a week, presented us with another large donation. It had taken us about six weeks but we had paid back the cost of having the leaflets printed and had almost two hundred and fifty pounds to give to Maria. Inna was due to visit Moscow on the 28th February 2004 and we celebrated by treating ourselves to a nice bottle of red wine and a few chocolate éclairs.

A couple of weeks earlier, just as we started our appeal, I had arranged to meet my mother in the city centre for a coffee. I didn't see her very often, we weren't that close, we both led our separate lives, meeting up now and then for a coffee and chat. We met on the 3rd February and during our chat I told her about Maria, the girl Inna and I were helping in Moscow. She suggested we contact Heather Mills-McCartney. Like most people, I had heard a little about Heather and I knew, from the newspapers and television, that she had married Paul McCartney. I had also heard that many years ago she had lost her leg in an accident involving a police motorcyclist. But that was about all I did know.

When I got home I told Inna about my mother's suggestion and a few days later I went to the library and looked up Paul McCartney in the Who's Who. It gave his record company address. That afternoon I wrote a letter to Heather and Paul McCartney, attaching to it one of our leaflets.

Paul and Heather McCartney
C/o MPL Communications Ltd
1 Soho Square, London, W1V6BQ
13th Feb 2004

Dear Paul and Heather,

I completely understand that you get many such requests for help and may never actually receive this letter, but if you do please take a little time to read the attached leaflet.

I am a writer and Journalist (NUJ Member XXXXX) and was based in Moscow for quite a while. Although I have now come back to the UK, my wife is Russian and we return frequently. I am still registered with the British Embassy. I won an award writing for IMPACT magazine about racism in Russia, and have had various other editorials published in magazines. My first book comes out next week. My wife Inna worked for a security company in Moscow until she moved with me back to the UK. We are perfectly genuine.

We met Maria begging outside a Metro near to where my wife worked. Her beauty in a harsh, hard world struck us. At first I wanted to write her story and then give her the proceeds from its sale, but at that time there was no interest from the British press, so we decided to start an appeal. Although, I must just mention, I still hope to write a book on her life, as it is a truly fascinating and remarkable tale.

Maria still has to beg to support herself and her son. She has little choice. As a disabled person she receives little support from the government in Russia and it is impossible for her to find work. Sadly Russia is not like the UK – there are virtually no provisions for the disabled.

Our aim is to give Maria and her son a better life, through education and support. Our long-term goal is to get Maria and her son a home of their own, and help Maria to get work. One day we would like to set up a small charity, helping others like Maria (we have an idea that Maria could do this with us).

Please feel free to contact us at any time. You are also more than welcome to visit us and to hear Maria's story in more detail or we can come to see you.

Thank you for your time Kindest regards

Robin and Inna Barratt

A week later Inna and I had decided to take an afternoon nap. We had worked late the previous night, finally getting to bed at about three am and the postman woke us up early that morning delivering a letter that needed signing for. Instead of going back to bed we both reluctantly got up, had breakfast and started work so by mid afternoon we were both feeling tired and a little lazy and decided to take a nap. Our thoughts and dreams started swirling around our minds as we started to fall asleep when the phone rang. I thought about letting it ring, but something compelled me to fight my initial impulse to lay there until it silenced and I got up off the bed and staggered over to the phone – we didn't receive many calls and I thought it was either someone that wanted to question us after receiving a leaflet through their letterbox or a double-glazing salesman – and then I would be really annoyed.

"Hello," I said sleepily.

"Hello, this is Heather Mills-McCartney."

I was suddenly wide awake, saying, and as loud as I could to get Inna's attention "Oh Hello Heather."

It was only after a few minutes chatting to Heather, and silently mouthing "Its Heather McCartney," that Inna also sat upright, attentive, inquisitive and very excited.

Miraculously Heather had received our letter. We spoke for quite a long time, we told her about Maria, how we met her and what had happened so far. Heather asked if Maria had ever had limbs. We told her she did but they were so old and uncomfortable she never wore them. Heather understood and promised that she would help. Heather and I discussed bringing Maria to the Dorset Prosthetic Clinic in the UK where Heather has close contacts. Heather would personally get Maria some really good artificial legs and cosmesis – the silicone cosmetic covering that made prosthetics so life-like. The legs, she said, would cost about five thousand pounds, the cosmetic covering about another five thousand. She promised she would also provide all the medical support needed to get her walking again. She told us about her charity and that it only provided support for victims of landmines, and so she said she would support and help Maria from her own personal finances and not via her charity.

I told Heather that Inna was actually flying to Moscow the following week. We didn't want to promise Maria something and then let her down so I asked Heather if this was definite, could we really talk to Maria about it. Maria had been through enough in her short hard life to have such wonderful promises made only to have them taken away. Heather confirmed everything – that she would definitely bring her to England and pay for brand new legs and yes, we could tell her. Heather gave me her personal mobile number, telling me to call her once Inna had seen Maria. Everything could then be planned.

We were ecstatic. That afternoon we couldn't stop smiling. With Heather's help we could change this girl's life. With legs she could walk and then maybe find a job and finally be the mother she so desperately wants to be.

We had been inclined to leaflet-drop near to where we lived; Trafford Road, Grove Road and various smaller roads off Ipswich road, but on the last Sunday before Inna was due to fly to Moscow we decided to leaflet along Newmarket Road and all the very wealthy adjoining roads. Altogether we had raised almost four hundred and fifty pounds from average income households, we felt absolutely sure that we would raise even more money by targeting the some of the biggest and wealthiest houses in Norwich. That Sunday we walked for almost three hours. We dropped leaflets through as many doors as we could. We went to Newmarket Road, Judges Walk, Mile End Rd, Mount Pleasant and almost all of Eaton. We had a week before Inna was due to fly to Moscow and hoped that we would get at least another couple hundred pounds. We waited, every day looking forward to the sound of letters hitting the doormat. Monday, Tuesday, Wednesday passed. Nothing. Not even one pound. Normally, and almost religiously, we would get at least two donations in the week following a day of leafleting. Letters would usually arrive on a Tuesday or Wednesday, or personally popped through our letterbox. Thursday's postman came and went, nothing, Friday arrived, again nothing. We were devastated. We already had some money for Maria but we had our hearts set on giving her more along with the wonderful news from

Heather. We had spent twice as long as normal, going to bigger houses, but nobody from any of these houses gave a single penny. They say the rich stay rich because they don't give, and on that day we certainly found that true. A little old lady living in a small one bedroom apartment round the corner from us personally came round with five pounds, all she had spare that week, while we were told to bugger off from the owner of one big house on Newmarket Road with a top of the range Mercedes and BMW smugly sitting in the drive. The cost of one tank of petrol for both those two vehicles would have given Maria a month's income.

Inna told me it was the same in Russia. It was the poor that helped the poor, the rich guarded their own wealth – they didn't know what it was like to be poor, and therefore didn't really care. The poor understood what it was like to be hungry, to be cold, to have nowhere to stay, to be afraid and lonely. The rich knew little about these things and therefore generally cared little, keeping within the sanctuary of their own sheltered, secure environment. I could not imagine that someone on Newmarket Road would ever consider spending their Sundays walking through the rain and the snow popping leaflets through their neighbour's letterbox in the hope of receiving a few pounds for someone they cared for and thought about and wanted to help. If the rich gave, they seemed to give reluctantly and without feeling. Throughout our appeal we even had visitors who had carefully bundled boxes of gifts – books, pencils, pens, school things for Anton or a nice blouse, some toiletries, a warm scarf for Maria. I could never imagine the rich spending their time over the kitchen table pondering what would be the best thing to buy. During the first six weeks we spent soliciting for donations, people who contacted us really cared, they cared for Maria and her son – two people they didn't know, had never met, and in a country two thousand miles away. This was incredible.

With the things we had been given for Maria, a few things we had bought, and some money, I drove Inna to Heathrow on the 28th February 2004. I had been booked to instruct on a Bodyguard training course in Iceland and we had decided that, while I was in Iceland, Inna might as well go back home to see her family and Maria again as well as renewing her visa. She was going to spend almost two weeks in Moscow. It had been a while since we had last been in contact with Maria and we felt sure she had forgotten us, putting us alongside other do-gooders that go back on their promises.

Like many Russian families, Inna and her family were close and she hadn't seen any of them since she left Russia in October so she was looking forward to going home. She missed them all; her mother's warmth and kindness, her father's sometimes idiosyncratic ways, her brother and his wife's constant bickering, her grandmother's occasional nagging, her grandfather's serenity, but most importantly she missed her dog. Inna loved animals; big or small, ugly or beautiful, she thought more for animals than she did for most people. Inna's favourite British television programme was Rolf Harris's "Animal Hospital." She would sit through most of it in tears. When she was just ten or eleven, to the horror of her parents, she turned up on the doorstep of her apartment clutching the most appallingly ugly and disheveled dog she had found scavenging for food nearby. She felt sorry for it and wanted to feed and look after it and was distraught for days when her parents wouldn't allow that dirty, smelly thing into the house.

February in Moscow would be mid-winter, the snow would be heavy and it would be minus fifteen, possibly lower. As far as we knew Maria was still begging and so we were both looking forward to knowing that she was all right. The day before Inna flew to Moscow I called Heather for the first time on the mobile number she had given us.

"Hello Heather, sorry to bother you," I said, "It is Robin here, we spoke last week regarding Maria. Just confirming everything is all right as Inna is off to Moscow tomorrow and will be meeting up Maria." I just wanted to verify that Heather hadn't changed her mind, that everything was still alright and that Heather was still going to provide Maria with new legs. Heather confirmed everything and yes we could tell Maria this wonderful, wonderful news.

I would be flying to Iceland from Stansted the day after Inna left for Moscow. After saying my farewells I drove back from Heathrow, had a few hours sleep and left bright and early the very next day. I had intended to catch the coach to Stansted, as it would have been a lot easier and far cheaper than driving and parking but when I checked the times on the internet taking the coach meant I had a three hour wait at the airport, which I didn't fancy, so I found a reasonably priced airport car park nearby.

Bodyguard training courses are always tough. They are tough for the students and even tougher for the instructors as we have to be seen to be able to do more, go further and for longer than the students. When the students are tucked up in bed exhausted from the days training, the instructors are generally planning the next day in detail. We then have to be up before everyone else, shouting and screaming that they're all late, even though we told them the night before that the day wouldn't start until six am and it was only five thirty. I was actually teaching on a nineteen day instructor's course, but I had agreed to only do ten days but felt that even those ten days were going to be a struggle. We were teaching hardened, experienced bodyguards and those fresh from the armed services and I wasn't as fit as I used to be, or as tough, or as strong willed.

Actually, I did enjoy teaching – if it was nine to five with an hour for lunch – but bodyguard training was sometimes extreme because of the extreme conditions many of the guys would eventually be working in and so it was essential to get them as prepared and equipped as possible, even though it almost killed the poor instructors.

Iceland wasn't the warmest of places at the best of times, with summer temperatures rarely exceeding eighteen to twenty degrees. I once remembered going to Iceland in September, thinking of all the gorgeous blond Icelandic women dressed in their skimpy summer dresses. It hailed almost all week. I wasn't impressed and vowed never to return, but I had. This trip was going to be my fourth or fifth.

As I arrived at Keflavik airport, about forty miles west of Reykjavik, I looked through the aircraft window at the bleak volcanic landscape of southern Iceland. It wasn't white, which I had expected, but it was sleeting heavily and the place looked miserable and depressed. They say that Iceland has one of the highest suicide rates in the world and, looking around, I could understand. The whole place looked bleak and unwelcoming, very little grows on the barren terrain – an occasionally stunted tree, a few artificially cultivated bushes. The centre of Iceland and all along its northern coast is said to be quite spectacular. Although I promised myself over and over again that I would take some time off to travel around the country, I never did and this visit was to be no exception. I was scheduled to return to the UK the day before Inna returned from Moscow.

Although a tough climate I have always found the

Icelandics extremely hospitable and very friendly and Reykjavik on a Friday and Saturday night puts even the most hardened party animal to shame. Probably all the pent-up frustration and boredom of living in such a bleak and inhospitable country manifests itself every weekend and Reykjavik city centre from about three to five am is like no other city centre in the world. Norwich at midnight pales into insignificance.

We had given the students some tasks and a project and, while the students did their research and preparation, Dan Sommer, Head of International Operations for the company, and I had some free time and headed for Reykjavik. As we were travelling into the town centre I told Dan about Maria.

"We make some of the best legs in the world," he said, matter-of-factly.

"Sorry," I replied, not really knowing what on earth he was talking about.

"Never heard of Össur?" he asked.

"No," I replied

"Össur is one of the biggest companies in Iceland and they make some of the best artificial limbs in the world. Let me call them, they might be interested in helping."

We swung off the road onto a side street and screeched to a halt, almost bumping into a huge 4 x 4 who had also decided to use his mobile phone. As Dan dialed Össur and spoke in Icelandic I stared up at the 4 x 4 parked next to us. Our little clapped out Ford looked tiny in comparison. When I first visited Iceland I wondered why many of the vehicles had their suspensions raised and were fitted with monstrous tyres. I thought everyone in Iceland had come from Essex and were on steroids. I actually laughed when I saw the first few jacked up, beefed up 4 x 4 and pickups, until an elderly man with his equally elderly wife got out from one and sauntered over to an ATM machine. And then it slowly dawned on me, it was the terrain that the vehicles were modified for, not some eighteen year old's inflated ego. Without the jacked up suspension and huge tyres much of Iceland would be inaccessible. I looked up at the driver and saw it was indeed it was an eighteen year old. He looked down at me, nodded as though to confirm what I had been thinking all along, and sped off.

Dan finished his conversation. Normally, in most languages, it's possible for me to understand at least a few words here and there, but not with Icelandic. The only thing I understood was "Heather Mills-McCartney". Even in Russia I could identify and recognize a few words here and there but Icelandic hasn't changed much since the ninth century when mainly the Norwegians settled for the first time on this small, cold, wet island. I have to ask, why?

"Tomorrow morning, ten am, we have an appointment with one of the directors."

Heather had already promised us her help, we trusted her completely and were really looking forward to working with her, but I somehow felt that if Össur could help as well it would give us a second option, just in case. In case of what, I didn't really know, but, having worked in the security industry for most of my life, having a contingency plan was what I instilled in everyone that trained with me. I always taught my students to ask "what if" and have a second plan as backup should the first in any way be compromised. With Heather *and* Össur's help our objectives and ambitions for Maria would certainly be a lot more achievable.

The students didn't have much of my attention that afternoon as my thoughts were pre-occupied with Össur and what I was going to tell them. I wanted to impress them with both the plight of Maria, but also with an idea of the problems and difficulties other disabled experience in Russia. Iceland seems even more advanced than England when looking after its disabled but the provisions the Russian government makes for its infirm must seem to come from the dark ages. In fact there are no facilities for the disabled at all. Absolutely nothing. Even getting out of most apartments for most disabled people was virtually impossible. Looking back, I don't think I ever saw one person in a wheelchair on the streets, not once. If you were disabled and it was possible to get out of your apartment with a wheelchair, most pavements were potholed, rutted, worn out and extremely dangerous. The attitude in Russia was that if you broke your leg falling down a hole in the path it was your fault for not looking, and not the government's fault for allowing the path to be kept in such an awful state of disrepair. And even if you did manage to overcome the obstacles of dilapidated paths, you could never cross the road – no one would stop for you, not ever. I have seen little old ladies barely able to walk forced to dash across roads to the sounds of screeching, blaring horns. Vehicles don't stop or slow down for anyone – being in the road means being in the way. And, if by some miracle you manage to get across the road, you could never get into the shops. Firstly there are almost always steps leading up into most stores, and then the isles and checkout are so tiny there is little space for humans let alone wheelchairs, and no one would ever dream of helping you. Customer service in most Russian shops is still almost non-existent. Retailers still take the old communist attitude that you are in their shop because you need something from them and not the other way round. They still cannot get round the idea that you are the customer and they need you and so shop assistants are still generally very unhelpful, rude and abrupt – most seem to think they can treat you exactly as they want. This is slowly changing, especially in the international stores in the centre of Moscow, but out in the poorer provinces where most of the disabled live, customer service simply does not exist.

And lastly, if you happen to be just about healthy and able enough to leave your wheelchair outside and walk round the supermarket, your chair definitely would not be there when you returned. It would have been stolen the minute you turned your back and struggled slowly through the supermarket doors.

Years ago, under communism, there were lots of government agencies working with and helping the disabled. By the end of the 1950s cooperatives of disabled people united over four thousand factories across all of Russia and employed over two hundred thousand disabled workers. However in 1956 the Communist Party nationalized most of these businesses and in 1960 the rest were disbanded. Ordinary disabled veterans, who lost their arms and legs on the battlefield, were sent to isolated places where no one could see them. After the fall of communism, and the race for prosperity and wealth, little regard was given to providing for the disabled. It was seen as simply a waste of money to build a ramp or other facilities for disabled access and most of the money allocated to rebuilding and renovating roads and paths quickly disappeared before it reached the pavement. I thought about the article I read in the Moscow Times a couple of years previously. It detailed a team of auditors sent in to audit money allocated from the government to services for the poor. It found that ninety five percent of the money simply disappeared. It could not be found. Only five percent of all the money allocated made its way to those that needed it the most. Most of it probably disappeared into the pockets of the government officials who allocated it in the first place. And because there was and still is no accountability and bribery and corruption extreme, the money could never be found. Even if an official was caught and found guilty, he would have probably siphoned away enough money to last a lifetime, and certainly more than enough to bribe any judge should he ever get taken to court.

That morning I awoke early, showered, shaved and put on my best trousers, shirt and tie. Because Dan and I were the only instructors that morning and he would have to take me into Reykjavik as our training camp was about thirty miles from Össur's office.

We generously gave the students the morning off but of course they had all woken up at six am, thinking we were playing our usual dirty tricks. But when they realised that we were also still fast asleep, they nervously went back to bed. But I am sure none of them actually slept until they heard the front door bang shut and the sound of our car in the distance. We were going to be a few hours. The base was about forty five minutes drive from the office; our meeting was at ten am. After the meeting Dan and I had arranged to pig-out at Burger King before we returned to the camp. We knew we wouldn't be back until about one pm and so had instructed the students to be ready to start at two.

Our appointment was with Mrs. Sigurborg Arnarsdóttir, who was the Manager of Treasury & Investor Relations. One of her jobs was to allocate funds and resources to non-profit and charitable projects. Dan and I sat in their grand boardroom waiting for Sigurborg and looking through Össur's brochure. One of the most striking images in their brochure was of a boy, probably around thirteen or fourteen years old, standing by the side of a swimming pool. He was wearing a blue, white and yellow Össur t-shirt; he was a double amputee, like Maria, loosing his legs just below the hip. But he stood with his two prosthetic legs in his Nike training shoes, hand on hip, looking confident, assured and happy. This is what Inna and I wished for Maria. We wished that we would someday see her standing in the same way.

Sigurborg came in apologizing for keeping us waiting. I looked at the clock on the wall above the MD's chair – she was about a minute late but apparently the Icelandics were extremely punctual. A colleague came in with Sigurborg and offered us coffee, which we gladly accepted. We weren't yet half way through the training course and the effects were already taking its toll. I could certainly do with yet another cup of coffee to help keep me awake. I too was hoping to have a morning off later in the week to sleep and recover. I was getting too old for this tough, hard life – all I now wanted was a cup of warm coco and my slippers near the fire.

Sigurborg sat in front of us and introduced herself. Like most Icelandics, her English was excellent. She had been working for Össur for quite a number of years. She told us that the company was named after its founder, Össur Kristinsson. An amputee himself, he studied prosthetics in Sweden before starting Össur in 1971. Back then the prosthetic industry was at its infancy and a comfortable prosthetic was virtually unheard of. Amputees simply could not lead a normal life. Össur Kristinsson's clinic took most of his time and so the evenings and weekends he spent looking for and developing new innovations and designs that would give the prosthetic wearer more comfort and allow him or her to lead a much fuller life. It was awarded its first patent in 1986. Össur are now well-known leaders in the field of prosthetics. Apart from its head office in Iceland, it also has offices in North America and Europe. I listened as she described their products, the FLEXI-FOOT prosthetic feet, the ICE-CROSS silicone liners, the amazing MAUNCH knee joints, which are used by amputee athletes. I thought about Maria pushing herself around on her little wooden platform and could never image that there were so many interesting innovations helping amputees. It was hard to believe that in a world of technology there are still people relying upon a block of wood, four rickety wheels and an old belt.

I spoke to Sigurborg, telling her all about Maria – her story and her plight. I also told Sigurborg about Heather's telephone call and involvement and her promises of support. I was really hoping that Össur would also help us. We sat chatting for about an hour when Sigurborg excused herself – she wanted to talk to her Director. We were brought another coffee and more cookies which were warmly welcomed as my stomach had started rumbling loudly. Dan and I sat quietly, looking around at the photographs on the wall. After about ten minutes Sigurborg returned and said they would be pleased to help. They would donate the limbs as long as Heather donated the cosmetic coverings, which she had already promised she would. It was fantastic news. I could go back to England and surprise Inna.

I must admit I spent the rest of the week not really concentrating on the students but on how things were going to develop with Maria and what was eventually going to happen. I day-dreamed that she was off the streets and walking and going to work every day, and coming home to her son and picking him up off the ground, and going to the cinema, and doing all the wonderful things she has never done. In my exaggerated and sometimes intense imagination I also had dreams that Inna and I were back in Russia running a little sanctuary for other disabled and infirm and destitute, offering them hope in a world of despair, offering them charity in world full of selfishness and greed.

After listening to Sigurborg talking about Össur and everything it could do for amputees I felt there was so much more to do after we had finished helping Maria.

There were so many more people to help. My head has always been full of dreams – I would imagine the most wonderful, unique scenarios and situations. I knew that some of my dreams were unattainable, unrealistic, but I dreamt them anyway. I knew that without dreams nothing would ever be achieved.

I got back to the UK the day before Inna was due to arrive home. It took me almost a day to sort through the mail and e-mails. I decided not to call Heather until Inna returned. I wanted to hear about her trip and the meetings with Maria. I cleaned the apartment and bought some flowers. Our apartment was tiny and sparsely decorated but it was nice to come home. I still enjoyed travelling but, more and more and as I got older, I would prefer the security of being at home, the familiarity of recognizable things, people and places.

Meeting Inna off the plane is always nice. Like me, she likes travelling and she really enjoyed going back to see her family and friends but she was also pleased to be returning to the UK, to her new home. She missed Moscow but in a virtual way, as, as soon as she arrived at the drab, depressive Sheremetyevo airport and after queuing for hours at passport control and inching her way through the surly customs and scrambling past the hordes of taxi hagglers and driving home in the impossible traffic past the rows and rows of dreary tenement blocks, she realised that there wasn't much to miss about the country after all. Her family was all that was really missed.

Inna had found Maria begging at her usual spot at the usual Metro station. She was huddled up against the cold, looking pretty miserable, but her eyes lit up and a beaming smile spread across her pretty face as soon as she saw Inna. She said she never expected to see her again, and it was a wonderful surprise.

Inna was with her grandmother. She had spoken to her at length about Maria and how we were helping her walk again. Perhaps she was a little suspicious, but certainly very intrigued and wanted to meet her. They all hugged and kissed and sat for a while huddled in the corner, chatting. Inna then arranged to meet Maria a few days later when she could bring her the presents and money we had raised.

When Inna and Maria met again up a couple of days later it wasn't snowing, but crispy clear. Inna took Maria to McDonalds and bought her a huge burger, large fries, strawberry shake and ice-cream. McDonalds was one of the only places in Moscow that actually had some facilities for the disabled. Every couple of months Maria would take Anton and they would sit together in a quiet corner having fun eating as much as they could afford. It was a real treat for them both. The Russians love their ice-cream. It can be minus twenty, snowing heavily, and they still wonder about enjoying a good ice-cream. I suppose one advantage is that it doesn't melt and your hands don't get sticky.

She gave Maria the money we had collected, and the clothes and toys for her son as well as a small bible given by Joyce, a member of Inna's Russian group. Maria was so grateful – she really didn't think she would ever see Inna again. The money, she said, would go towards helping to pay for kindergarten and the bible she would take with her everywhere, it will help protect her.

While they sat looking out to the snowy pavement, Inna spoke to her about Heather, without actually mentioning Heather's name. She said that she had met a "wealthy" woman very keen on helping Maria walk again. Inna said that this "wealthy" woman had also lost a leg and had some very good contacts in that field of medicine and she could get Maria some very good new legs. Maria was excited and extremely interested, listening to Inna intently as she slurped and sucked at her milk shake. Maria explained that she already had artificial legs. A couple of years earlier, thinking legs would be better than her platform and not knowing any better, Lydmilla more or less forced Maria to attend a clinic where the government gave her prosthetics. The doctors were rude and clumsy and the examination painful. The legs she was given made her bleed and bruise and she had to fix them onto her torso with awful leather straps, which meant she couldn't even use the toilet without taking her legs off. They were so uncomfortable and clumsy and old she rarely wore them – only on a few rare occasions. She preferred to remain on her wooden platform. Inna tried to explain that these legs would be different, that the woman helping her knew and understood that if she had uncomfortable legs she would never wear them and so she would only provide new, comfortable legs. Maria didn't believe it was possible. She had only seen old Soviet style prosthetics and couldn't understand that there were other types but she reluctantly nodded and agreed. If indeed it was possible then it would be wonderful, but she knew it wasn't.

Inna used the rest of the money to buy Maria a mobile phone. In that way it would be possible for us to keep in more regular contact, especially important as things began to develop. We would need to talk to Maria in order to update and arrange everything. She wouldn't need to call us, but we needed to be able to call her, so she would have nothing to pay on the phone herself.

Maria seemed more confident with us and our promises. She understood we were serious about her and cared for her and had devoted our time in raising money for her. She still couldn't believe it, she simply could not believe that people in another country so far away actually cared for her and her son and really wanted to help.

Inna understood that Maria desperately wanted to do something with her life. Maria dreamt about being able to help others too. Other "street" people often came to her asking advice or seeking help. She enjoyed trying to work out other people's problems, trying to help them around difficult situations, being there for them. Her life was harsh and hard but she wasn't just preoccupied with her own survival, she cared for others around her. She wanted to be a good mother, not a mother that begged at a dirty Metro station, but a mother her son can one day look up to with pride, a mother that will one day do wonderful things.

There was sincere emotion in Maria's eyes as they said their farewells. She didn't cry, she had long since hardened herself to the traumas of life begging on the streets, but she saw there was new hope. Inna warned told her that these things might take a long time, and they might not actually happen. Maria knew this, she understood that the world is full of false hopes, but she still preferred to hope than to have nothing.

With Heather's involvement and Össur's donation we were doubly motivated to raise more money and so, when Inna returned from Moscow we resumed our Sunday march round the streets popping leaflets through letter boxes and waiting for an occasional cheque on our doormat.

On the 29th March both Össur and Heather's personal assistant contacted us by e-mail asking for some photos of Maria so they can gauge her level of disability.

Mon, 29 Mar 2004 09:06
From: RobinBarratt@yahoo.com
To: Heather Mills-McCartney and Össur

Hello
Please find attached three images of Maria – I have a few more if interested.

We spoke to Maria today, she is so excited about the future and is looking forward to meeting you and passes on her regards. She asked us to thank you for everything.

Regards

Robin and Inna

The day after sending the images to Heather we had a bombshell. Sonya wrote to us telling us that she was having problems getting Dorset Orthopaedic to agree to carry out the fitting of the limbs for Maria. She said that the Dorset Orthopaedic already had their charitable budget taken up for the next couple of years and it was doubtful whether they would have any more funds available.

By that time we hadn't actually told Heather about Össur's agreement to help, as we wanted to keep that as a contingency plan – just in case. We didn't expect anything to go wrong, as we believed Heather and her promises and commitment to Maria. She had confirmed everything twice by telephone before Inna left for Moscow, and Heather had assured us that we could tell Maria what she had promised – that Heather had pledged to sponsor Maria from her own funds and not via the charity.

We felt sure that this was just a mistake, a slight misunderstanding or some kind of confusion in communication between Sonya and Heather.

31 Mar 2004 16:26

From: "Robin Barratt" robinbarratt@yahoo.com

Subject: Re: Images of Maria attached

To: "Sonya Mills" sonya@heathermillsmccartney.com

I was surprised to receive your e-mail, as Heather personally called us pledging her support and help. Heather told us to speak to Maria and start to organize everything. She said she would do this off her own back and not via her charity. Please speak to her about this urgently and call us back as soon as possible as we simply cannot go back to Maria with this news after Heather's promise to her.

Regards

We were stressed and worried and upset that we might have to go back to Maria and tell her that the promises we had made, and that our "wealthy lady" had made, had now been withdrawn. Maria had begun talking about a new life, a life like everyone else, proud, fulfilled, happy. I sent Sonya, Heather's personal assistant, another e-mail telling her of Össur's involvement, telling her that Heather could now save some money as Össur had agreed to supply the limbs and that Jamie Gillespie, their prosthetist based in the UK, would fit them. Because I managed to get Össur to provide limbs we had saved Heather at least five thousand pounds, quite possibly a lot more. Now all Heather needed to pay for were the medical expenses, Maria's expenses of coming to the UK and the cosmetic covering.

A day or so later we heard back from Sonya. Apparently there had been some kind of "misunderstanding," and that Heather was indeed funding the project independently. We were told that they were in the process of working out the costs of the project and that they would liaise with Össur regarding organization and logistics. We both smiled again and breathed a huge sigh of relief. Sonya told us that the project would take two weeks from start to finish and that Maria would have to stay in Hampshire near the Dorset Clinic. Sonya asked if we could send them photographs of Maria's residual limbs which they would then pass onto the clinic. We were then asked what budget we had for Maria's travel and accommodation and whether we had already made any arrangements.

The reply was nothing like Heather's original telephone call. Heather had originally told us that *she* would bring Maria over to the UK and cover all the expenses of having new legs fitted and Inna and I had genuinely thought that this was what she was going to do. It would have been impossible for us to save the money needed to pay for Maria's flight and two weeks accommodation. It would probably cost at least a thousand pounds, possibly a lot more and we simply did not have that much money and it would be doubtful if we could raise that much either. It was four in the morning and I couldn't sleep with the worry of everything. I felt I had to write back and so I got up out of bed, turned on the PC and wrote a reply.

Date: Fri, 2 Apr 2004 04:37
From: "Robin Barratt" robinbarratt@yahoo.com
Subject: Re: Images of Maria attached
To: "Sonya Mills" sonya@heathermillsmccartney.com

Sonya
We shall try and speak to Maria and ask if she has photos of her limbs, otherwise, short of Inna flying out there herself and taking the photos, we wouldn't know how to go about getting them. Or Maria can wait until the end of this month when she sees Össur's Prosthetist in Moscow.

Regarding Maria's accommodation. When Heather first called us she told us that she would fly Maria to the UK, where she would stay at a guest house near the Dorset clinic which is where most of the patient's of the clinic stay and is especially designed for this purpose. She also said she had contacts within the

Russian government to help with passports, visa etc. In her own words she said she "speaks to Putin often". Heather promised us that she will commit herself to this project, personally and not through her charity.

Heather also said that she would fly to meet Maria during Heather's visit to St Petersburg. This was great news as we are not wealthy and could not finance any of this project ourselves. We called Heather just before Inna flew to Moscow to see Maria, just to confirm everything as we obviously did not want to promise something to Maria that we couldn't fulfill. This would simply be awful. Heather confirmed everything the second time, that yes she will provide all the support needed to get Maria walking again and that Inna can tell Maria this in Moscow and start to make arrangements to get Maria a passport etc. Heather also asked us to find someone in Moscow that could provide ongoing support to Maria once she returns, which we managed to do, the Private Russian – American Family Clinic. Inna spoke to the chief Orthopaedist who confirmed he would be able and pleased to work with us.

I realize that there may be a little confusion, as your last e-mail said that the Dorset clinic were unable to provide limbs, and now you are asking where Maria will stay and what funds we have.

We are not rich and cannot fund this ourselves. We will only just be able to afford to fly Inna out to Moscow so she can be with Maria when she visits Össur's Prosthetist. This was why we were extremely happy when Heather called and offered her support, and when she confirmed all of this before Inna flew to Moscow to see Maria.

To help with the cost of this, as you know, I managed to get a commitment from Össur to supply the limbs – which they have agreed to do.

We have not bothered Heather, preferring to deal through yourself, so please relay this information back to Heather. She must be busy and speak to many people so I understand the confusion.

We look forward to your reply concerning the above.

Thanks again

Later that Friday afternoon we got a reply. According to Sonya, Heather was apparently out of the country and not easily contactable which was what caused the initial confusion, but she was indeed still committed. Sonya told us that she had already made contacts with a couple of people regarding flights and was waiting to hear back from them. She asked us which airport would be easier for Maria to fly from, and who would be coming with Maria because they wanted to know how many tickets they would need. Would her son be coming, and a helper? And what about Maria's visa? Had we started to make arrangements with the British Embassy in Moscow as they had someone in their office who could start on Maria's visa application.

We felt a little bewildered. We didn't really know what was happening. Heather had said one thing and yet time and time again Sonya, kept saying something completely different. We then had an e-mail from Össur regarding their prosthetist visit to Moscow. This was great news as Össur had already started to plan everything and things, with them, were quickly put in motion. Literally just a few weeks after I had visited them at their office in Iceland they promised us new legs for Maria and they had now started to honor their promise, without question, hesitation, doubt. This was fantastic.

With a copy to us, Sigurborg at Össur had written to Sonya confirming their involvement.

To: "Sonya Mills" sonya@heathermillsmccartney.com
CC: jgillespie@Össur.com, irichter@Össur.com,
robinbarratt@yahoo.com
Subject: Re: no subject
From: sarnarsdottir@Össur.com

Dear Sonya.
Sorry I have not answered you before. I was waiting for a confirmation from Jamie (the Prosthetist) when he would be in Moscow.

Mr. Jamie Gillespie, prosthetist, will be in Moscow from April 24-28. As I told Robin we need to see Maria and evaluate her condition before we can say anything about what kind of products would suit her. As Maria was amputated many years ago and has not used any artificial limbs there is a possibility that her muscles in the residual limbs are too week and her hip-joints could be too stiff to be able to make use of our products. If Maria is able to use prosthesis we have a large range of products and therefore we would be able to provide suitable products.

Our suggestion is that Jamie will meet Maria in Moscow and following their meeting we know what possibilities Maria has to be fitted. Jamie could either meet her at Dorset Orthopaedic or at one of our distributors work shop. Which would suit you better?

Best Regards.
Sigurborg Arnarsdóttir
Manager of Treasury & Investor Relations ÖSSUR HF

So we knew that Jamie was going to Moscow and would definitely be seeing Maria. I now had to book Inna's flight so that she could be there at the same time as Jamie. We had hardly any money ourselves as Inna wasn't working and I was struggling to support us both. There were some weekends when Inna and I had to survive on porridge as we hadn't any money to buy food. But we did have a few pounds we had raised from leaflets and we just about managed to scrape up the rest of the money to buy Inna's ticket. We were both really excited – we couldn't actually believe things were progressing so quickly. From the initial idea of just giving Maria some money we had now managed to not only raise money but hopefully one day very soon get her walking properly again for the first time in her life.

Date: Sun, 18 Apr 2004 20:57
Subject: Maria
To: robinbarratt@yahoo.com
CC: sarnarsdottir@Össur.com, irichter@Össur.com,
sonya@heathermillsmccartney.com
From: jgillespie@Össur.com

Robin,
I'm heading out to Russia in the morning (Monday 19th April) and will be in the country until the 28th April. I will be in Moscow from the 24-28th April and hope to meet with Maria during this time. During my time in Russia I will be working with our local business partner who also assists with translation. Our business partner also arranges accommodation during my visit and I'll be able to provide you with my hotel details in Moscow within the next day or so. My time in Moscow is limited and during the day I will be attending a rehabilitation conference. An evening meeting would be preferred if this is possible. I'm looking forward to the opportunity to meet with Maria during my visit having heard so much about this remarkable young lady. Please feel free to contact me on my mobile phone number below during my visit to discuss the meeting with Maria. As soon as I know my hotel details I'll forward these on to you.
Kind Regards
Jamie Gillespie
Prosthetist – International Markets
Össur Prosthetics

Jamie finally managed to get to Moscow, after a delay with his visa. The Russian Embassy in London has been voted by the expat community as the rudest of all the Russian Embassies anywhere in the world. You would have thought that working in an Embassy, in a wonderful area of London, with a good salary would make the Embassy staff friendlier, happier and more helpful, but it has somehow made them worse. They are rude and arrogant and abrupt and treat everyone with disdain and contempt. I have been to the embassy a few times, queuing up early outside in all weathers. There is no guard or assistant manning the outside gate, answering questions, helping out, but a heavy metal turnstile that automatically lets in a few "victims" at a time. The attitude at that Embassy dates back to communism, people are nothing and should be treated as nothing. Apparently there was one thing wrong with Jamie's visa application and so he was turned away. This delayed his trip a few days, but finally he managed to get the right documents and his passport was finally stamped.

I sent another e-mail to Sonya just to confirm that Inna was on her way to Moscow and briefly detailed the problem that Maria would have getting to the UK.

Mon, 19 Apr 2004 07:53:33
From: "Robin Barratt" robinbarratt@yahoo.com
To: "Sonya Mills" sonya@heathermillsmccartney.com
Subject: Reply

Thanks Sonya
Hope you had a good break.
    Inna is flying to Moscow Thursday to help Maria meet Jamie. We had an e-mail from him last night. Because Maria does not

have registration, or a job, we are having problems getting her an international passport. We will keep you updated.

Regards

Robin

Chapter 10

To Moscow, again

We managed to scrape enough money together for Inna's flights and she flew out to Moscow on Thursday 22nd April. She would try to contact Jamie as soon as she arrived, as we hadn't yet received Jamie's contact details or the address of the hotel where he would be staying. But Inna had a mobile phone and we sent an e-mail to Jamie with Inna's contact details so either he could call her directly, or he could contact me and I would then forward his details to her.

Jamie had quite a busy week in Russia as Össur was trying to develop close contacts with other prosthetic companies and so most of Jamie's time was spent in meetings and lecturing at conferences. It was going to be a touch and go as to whether Inna could get Maria to meet Jamie, as she were not going to know until the very last minute exactly when Jamie was going to be in Moscow or where he was going to be staying. Inna then had to contact Maria and arrange to get her to Jamie. Inna felt sure that Maria would be begging at her normal place, but it wasn't definite, things could have changed since she had last spoken to her. Inna had tried calling her a couple of times, but her phone was turned off. Finally and at the last minute, Inna had managed to get hold of Maria and at more or less the same time Jamie had contacted Inna. He told her that he would be arriving by train from Saratov, about four hundred miles south east of Moscow, where he had been at a conference. As the train took most of the day to reach Moscow he arranged to meet Maria and Inna late in the afternoon at hostel Voshod where Maria lived.

Inna made her way to the run-down hostel and called Maria from the lobby. Maria came down with Valery, her friend and helper. Although Maria seemed a little nervous they hugged and kissed. Inna and Maria had become friends, Maria felt that Inna cared for her and every meeting was a joy. Shortly after Inna arrived at the hostel Jamie also arrived in a taxi direct from the train station. This was the first time Inna had met Jamie and she immediately warmed to him. She expected someone older and was pleasantly surprised when he got out from the taxi. He was only around thirty years old, warm and friendly and immediately very caring and sympathetic. He was with Maryana, who at that time represented Össur in Russia. They sat in a small Russian style café adjacent to the lobby of the hotel and introduced themselves to each other. Maria was very nervous and sat quietly next to Inna, tightly holding her hand. After a few minutes of getting to know each other and pleasantries they all then went to Maria's room. Jamie first examined her old Russian legs. He shook his head in despair, "no wonder they were so uncomfortable," he remarked looking at the old worn out "medieval" sockets and liners. Jamie took out his laptop, plugged it into the wobbly two-pin wall socket and showed Maria the products that Össur would be providing. Maria stared at the screen, fascinated. He showed her pictures of all the components of the prosthetic legs and how they are all put together as well as before and after images of other amputees. Jamie also asked if Maria had any objections to any publicity, as Össur wanted to put Maria's Story onto their website. Maria said no, she didn't mind at all.

Back in the UK I nervously sat by the phone all afternoon while Jamie met Maria. Inna had sent me a text telling me Jamie was on his way and that she would call me when they finally finished. I sat and waited, wondering what was going on, what was being said, how Maria was, and whether it was in fact possible to have new legs. Depending upon the actual disability it wasn't always possible to have prosthetics. There's a wide range of factors that can influence prosthetic prescription. From our discussions with Jamie and a little research on the internet it seemed that the general health of the patient is always considered first and foremost. For some frail patients it is sometimes better not to wear prosthetics, as they could prove too difficult to manage and control, but we knew that Maria was in good health, she had to be fairly healthy and fit to work on the streets as she did. No one in poor health could easily survive the Russian winters. We also wanted Maria to believe that these new legs would make her life so much easier and much more comfortable. Maria was now accustomed to mobility on her platform and getting her to commit to a period of lower mobility when learning to use the prosthesis might not appeal to her. Also the condition and length of her residual limbs could also influence the choice of prosthetic used. Shorter, scarred and sensitive residual limbs are more of a challenge to fit successfully.

As I sat at home in the UK while Maria had her initial consultation with Jamie, and hoping that Inna would call as soon as she could, I thought back to sitting in the board room at Össur and listening to how prosthetics have developed since Össur first formed the company over thirty years ago. Many cases that have proved to be difficult in the past can now be successfully managed by a medical team, but the key player was always the prosthetic user themselves and we hoped that Maria was willing and able to commit to a program of walking re-education and adaptation if she was to use the prostheses successfully and eventually return to walking.

Finally Inna called. She told me how Maria had been completely bowled over by Jamie's care and understanding. When they first met, Maria was quite nervous and expected a lot of pain and discomfort, as that is what she normally got after visiting the Russian clinic and prosthetist, but there was no discomfort and no pain, no harsh treatment and rudeness – she couldn't believe how gentle and kind Jamie was through the whole examination. Inna translated as Jamie carefully measured her limbs and examined her back and pelvis. Maria's residual limbs were in good condition, and the length of each limb was about fifteen centimetres. She had good muscle strength too, but she had a marked scoliosis (curvature) of the spine and her rib cage had gradually rotated from the years spent on her wooden platform pushing herself around with her wooden block. This didn't cause her any pain but it did concern Maria when they discussed her assessment. Jamie had asked Maria what she really wanted from her new prosthetics. She said she really, really wanted her legs to look like Heather Mills-McCartney's. She was inspired and encouraged by Heather, she wanted to be like her in every way – her strength and beauty motivated Maria to want new legs more than ever. But she didn't want to be uncomfortable. Like any young woman of her age, Maria also really wanted to wear high heels. She wanted to wear skirts or tight jeans. She wanted to feel like a real woman. She wanted to walk and sit and get into and out of a car easily. She wanted to be able to use a train or a bus. And above all she wanted to walk with her son, holding his hand, looking down at him. Inna and I felt so pleased that everything had gone smoothly and that both Jamie and Maria seemed happy. This was the first stage and it had

gone incredibly well. If things hadn't, our dreams for
Maria and Maria's dreams would have disappeared, but so
far things were looking good, although as I was to find
out, it was certainly not going to be like that in the months
to come.

It took a while for us to receive Jamie's report as he had to
fly to Mexico directly after his stay in Moscow. Every day
we looked at our e-mail inbox, hoping that he would have
the time to reply, and finally, almost three weeks after he
saw Maria he returned to the UK and sent his summarised
report to us via email.

Date: Wed, 12 May 2004 17:32
To: "Robin Barratt" robinbarratt@yahoo.com
Subject: Re: Maria
From: jgillespie@Össur.com

Hi Robin,
I've only just returned from Mexico which ends a month of travelling. I'm now going to be in the UK until the end of May.

It was great to meet with Maria and Inna during my visit. My
trip to Russia was very busy and time was a little short but I collected all the information I required and completed the report on
trains in Russia while travelling.

I'll have to send you the report on CD as the file is large.
The pictures I took were in high resolution and are far too large
to send via e-mail. Can I please have an address to send this
CD to?

All in all I see no problems in working with Maria from a clinical point of view. There is quite a marked scoliosis of her spine
and if anything prostheses may help to prevent this condition
from worsening. Although it won't be easy for Maria to use her
prostheses in terms of high energy expenditure we can make her

as comfortable as possible with good sockets and very good prosthetic components. Maria appears very well motivated to use comfortable limbs and that's very important. This will be a team effort and Maria is the key person in this team.

I have some thoughts that I'd like to share with you. Some of these are just me thinking out loud but I'd like to hear your comments. Only some of these comments will be added to my report.

It seems as if Maria will have huge difficulty in travelling to the UK and that the prosthetic service will need to be carried out in Russia. I'm interested if Heather Mills -McCartney will still be prepared to provide assistance if this is not carried out at Dorset Orthopaedic.

If work will be carried out in Russia we can help find people who we would suggest carry out this work. If carried out in Russia I would make sure I'm available to lend a hand and make sure the best possible outcome is achieved. Many of the products from Össur are not so well known currently in Russia as many local products are used. The concepts and products are not 'plug and play' as in you cannot pull these off a shelf and use them effectively, they require good understanding of biomechanics and also modern socket concepts.

Maria's lifestyle. I accept that the prostheses provided will not be used full time due to increased energy expenditure and slower mobility than as now. At this level of amputation it is very difficult to use prostheses full time. By providing prostheses I understand that it's hoped Maria can change her profession. Her current lifestyle seems comfortable and I wonder if the prostheses will cause financial problems during transition between careers. If this is the case it may be easier to continue as now with an income. I would like to hear your views here.

It's hoped that any prostheses provided will be covered financially by Össur and Heather Mills McCartney. There is the question of future sockets (section of the prostheses moulded precisely to the residual limb). It's expected that within months slight adjustments will be required which is not unusual after long periods of non prosthetic use. These adjustments will increase comfort as small changes occur. Overtime however following these changes new sockets will be required; again this is usual for all limb users. The time before new sockets are required cannot be stated as there are many factors which would influence this. My question here is who will carry out these adjustments and new sockets. My concern is that over time if working with local prosthetist the socket design may slowly evolve back to the situation as now with the crucial alignment also not being followed. I'm hoping that if I have the opportunity to work with local prosthetist I can also educate them at the same time. We then have to hope they follow similar procedures next time.

Gait training. The prostheses that will be provided are some of the best in the world and to be able to use this as effectively as possible some gait training is required. I am aware that this is not a big thing in Russia following prosthetic delivery. Do you know of anyone in Moscow who could help here? This training is on-going and cannot be carried out in one session.

It would be great to get the opportunity to meet up if you find yourself in London. I'll be around until the end of the month before I head out and about again.

Let me know if there's anything else I can do to support this.

Thanks

Jamie Gillespie

Prosthetist

International Markets Össur Prosthetics

Inna wanted to reply to Jamie personally, as it was she that met him and had spend a while with Maria, getting to know her and understanding her needs and goals and ambitions. (Edited excluding most of the original questions but Inna's use of English has been left exactly as written)

Sat, 15 May 2004 08:31:30
From: "Robin Barratt" robinbarratt@yahoo.com
Subject: Re: Maria – reply to your letter
To: jgillespie@Össur.com

Hello, Jamie,

Sorry for not replying sooner. We were away for a few days. It would be very good to meet up with you sometime at the end of May before you go on another trip.

It was great to meet you in Moscow. Maria liked you very much. She told me afterwards that none of the doctors she knows so far had been so kind, gentle and considerate to her.

It is great news too that Maria is prepared both physically and mentally to have new and comfortable prostheses. She does need them and they will make her life much easier though she is not the person to complain much.

Below under your comments you will find our thoughts and feelings with regards to what is going to happen to Maria.

"It seems as if Maria will have huge difficulty in travelling to the UK"

We do not think that there will be some problems in this regard. Sonya, Heather's PA, made some inquiries about the possible costs of having Maria's new limbs fit in Moscow. As you know I found a clinic in Moscow which is ready to put her in and provide all the necessary therapy and rehabilitation facilities. It is called the American-Russian Family Medical Clinic. Again if it happens in Moscow perhaps you will be able to fly again with me to meet the personnel of that clinic and assess their facilities. You will probably be able to provide some initial training so that the doctors could help Maria to get used to the limbs on the on-going basis. Initially we had Heather's commitment to support Maria as even in the case Maria has her prostheses fit in Dorset she would need some help on her coming back as she would not be able to stay in England during the indefinite period. We believe we should do things one step at a time though again we do have a Heather's word to help us.

"If work will be carried out in Russia we can help find people who we would suggest carry out this work"

We do rely upon you and your experience in this regard. We do not know much about all those things so your assistance would be greatly appreciated. And even if it takes place in Dorset we hope to be able to arrange your visit to Moscow so you could help Maria with her "first few steps" and having a contact with that clinic we want to introduce them to you and you to them in any case.

"Maria's lifestyle. I accept that the prostheses provide will not be used full time due to increased energy expenditure and slower mobility than as now"

Well this is quite a difficult point. I talked to Maria many times about her life, her goals, what she wants to do so that we can understand better where and how we can help her. In the first place we are determined to help her with artificial limbs notwithstanding whether she is going to continue like this or not. As at this stage we cannot simply turn our backs and tell her that we are sorry but because she is comfortable (might be comfortable, as we know she is not) with her current state of things we decided not to help her with prostheses. We believe that in any case new comfortable legs will help her considerably to feel more confident about her life. There have been a few changes in Maria's life. She managed to get the official registration of the Moscow region. It means she can officially apply for a job. She also won a trial with a relative who deprived her of her room in the apartment thus making her homeless. So now she has a place to live in. It is not in Moscow but in that village – about an hour by train from Moscow. She told me that she detest begging on the streets but she does it because she needs money for renting a room at the hostel and the money to send her son though he is more or less comfortably provided by his God mother. She also needed to save money for buying new prostheses. With our help she would not need to beg to buy new limbs. Again she told me she would be quite happy living in that small village on her small pension. Plus she wanted to find a job. With her new legs it would not be that difficult though it is a long- term ambition. Again, she is young, pretty. She obviously wants to get married and have more children. With her new legs she may start going out as it is obvious that sitting in that underpass she would not meet some eligible man who would love her and take care of her. We also cannot exclude this possibility. So despite her apparent comfort with the present situation she is not comfortable about it inside. She is just an optimist and she believes that if she works hard now the day will come when she will be happy in her own home with the family she craves to build. She strongly believes that the begging is just a temporary stage in her life as she is not a beggar by nature she wants more from her life. And we think she is the one who deserves it.

"It's hoped that any prostheses provided will be covered financially by Össur and Heather Mills McCartney"

We believe that having Heather's commitment we will be able to solve this. You do work with Russia. So we do not think it will be that difficult to travel there from time to time to follow Maria's progress. Again we will develop good contacts with that Moscow clinic where they will provide assistance. Because it is quite a modern western owned medical center they should be up to date with the modern technologies and it won't be that hard for you to train them to help Maria efficiently.

"Gait-training. The prostheses that will be provided are some of the best in the world and to be able to use this as effectively as possible some gait training is required"

See the above comment. And we can also ask your Russian partners as they might definitely know somebody because they do operate in this field.

Again we want to stress so that there is not any misunderstanding. We talked to Heather and she insisted that she wants to help Maria and we will see by ourselves that this support will be ongoing and not one time. Heather does know that getting and wearing prostheses is not a one-day task and perhaps you can also stress this in your report to them, when we spoke to her she obviously understood that she was going to commit herself to this on an ongoing basis whenever her help and assistance is required.

Also because we are slowly building up Maria's Fund we are also determined to help her.

Where we are at the moment. The state of things is as follows. On your side we are waiting for the report and Össur's and Heather's reaction to it. On Maria's side we are on stand-by as she being helped by her friend is going to apply for an international passport. We will definitely know it by the mid of June. Plan A is to do everything in Moscow. Plan B, if she gets the passport, to fly her to Dorset and do everything here. Either way we would like to ask both Össur and / or Heather to fly you to Moscow with me and start working with Maria's there, visit the clinic etc.

Hope this all makes sense. We look forward to your report, once we have this we can then go forward as quickly as we can. Feel free to call us at anytime, look forward to seeing you again soon.

Inna

A few days earlier, on the 10th May Inna had written another e-mail to Sonya and Heather, as well as forwarding the reply to Jamie's email.

From: Robin Barratt robinbarratt@yahoo.com
Date: Mon, 10 May 2004 16:39
To: Sonya Mills sonya@heathermillsmccartney.com,
Heather@heathermillsmccartney.com
Subject: Re: Maria

Hello, Sonya
Here is the latest update from Inna on Maria's story.

On April 28th, together with Jamie Gillespie we went to see

Maria for her first medical assessment. I am not going to get into medical details as Jamie will send you the complete and full report. Maria is in good condition both physically and mentally. Jamie checked her limbs and muscles and said that they were strong enough and could not see anything that could prevent Maria from wearing artificial limbs.

Maria has a strong character and she is determined to wear prosthetics as long as they are good ones. We saw her old artificial limbs and can understand perfectly why she cannot wear them. They look and feel simply awful. She told us that they are so uncomfortable that she can wear them only a couple of hours at a time. After that she experiences pain and discomfort, her limbs become bruised and the skin on them irritated. Additionally they have so many belts to secure them on her limbs that she cannot even go to the toilet while wearing them!! She was very impressed by what prosthetics Össur can make for her. It would change her life completely. She would be able to wear normal clothes, feel comfortable all the time while wearing them and most important she would not need to worry that she can fall and collapse every minute. Again the full report will be sent to you by Jamie who I believe is in Mexico at the moment. He is due to come back in a week's time. He has all the pictures together with his medical assessment and suggestions about what type of the prosthetics she will need.

Now about where the limbs will be fitted. At the moment Maria's friend is trying to get a foreign passport for her. Through the court she managed to now get the Moscow regional registration and now she can apply to get a passport. She will know where she has got or not got her passport by the mid of June. Then if she does we can perhaps fly her to England. If she does not then we will do everything in Moscow. Jamie said he would like to fly there with me and start fitting. I also found a Moscow based western type clinic called Russian American Family Medical Center. I talked to the Head of Orthopaedic Department Dr. Vladimir Kolesov. He told me that of course at first they would need to see Maria and her new prosthetics but generally they have all the facilities there for a successful rehabilitation period.

The contact details of the center are as follows:

Moscow, 2nd Tverskoy-Yamskoy lane, 10

Direct telephone number to reach Vladimir Kolesov: 007-095-251-52-97

e-mail: mediclub@cityline.ru

www.mediclub.ru http://www.mediclub.ru/

The cost of staying in the center is as follows:

Double room (including all the meals and care facilities) 140 Euros per night.

Physical-therapy, special massages and medical procedures are for an additional price. As far as we explained what Maria would need, we were told that it could be another 50-100 Euros per day maybe a little more. Totally the price might be up to 250 – 300 EURO a day (200 GBP) including everything.

When we initially talked to Heather she said that she would love to meet Maria in June during the visit of Sir Paul McCartney and herself to St. Petersburg. I told Maria about that. On her side she would be delighted to meet Heather as she wanted to thank her personally for helping her and giving her a new start in life. I told Maria about Heather and her loss of a leg and Maria was impressed by her personality and strength.

Will you let us know if Heather still wants to meet Maria and we can try to arrange it?

So that is where we stand at the moment. It is wonderful that slowly we are achicving what we first dreamed about and, with you, Heather and Össur, we can get Maria off that horrible wooden platform and walking properly again.

Please pass this onto Heather and let me have your views as soon as you can.

Kindest regards as always

Robin and Inna

Over a week later we heard back from Sonya. Heather was feeling good about the fact that Maria was being fitted in Moscow. This would certainly make things a lot easier for everyone concerned, especially Maria. Maria had never left Russia, let along travelled on an airplane, plus she didn't speak a word of English.

Sonya said that Heather wanted to know what treatment Maria would need at Russian American Family Medical Centre and roughly how long would she be expected to stay? This confused me a little, as it was only a short while ago that Sonya had informed us that the treatment would take about two weeks. They must have fitted hundreds if not thousands of artificial legs so surely they knew exactly what treatment Maria would be having? I wasn't a prosthetist, and knew nothing about the industry but I couldn't image that things would be that drastically different in Russia than the other countries in which Heather Mills-McCartney's charity work. Sonya also asked how close to the clinic Maria lived as normally in England amputees generally do not stay at the clinic but have appointments every few days, and gait training is usually done whilst visiting the clinic. Physiotherapy is usually something that most new amputees will also have.

Heather also wanted to know a little more about Jamie. She asked where he was based, does he work for Össur, was he a qualified prosthetist and does he personally do fittings? She asked about the limbs that Jamie will be recommending as, at that time, Heather was unaware of any high leg amputee wearing artificial legs without body straps. Heather seemed intrigued about the new developments Össur were having in that field and how it would benefit the work she was doing with other amputees.

Sonya also mentioned that Heather would really like to

see Maria while she was with her husband Paul in St. Petersburg, Russia, but it really depended on time and her daughter Beatrice. They wanted to know whether Maria could get to St. Petersburg to meet her. She apologized for so many questions, but confirmed again that they have a budget and many people to help and they had to account for every penny.

Yet again I was slightly troubled at Sonya's reply. I completely understood that they need to know costs and that they were interested in Jamie's background and his qualifications, but Sonya was yet again speaking as though the charity and not Heather herself was financing the project. We were, of course, always conscious of costs and had literally saved Heather thousands of pounds by getting Össur to provide the limbs and Jamie's time, but I could not understand why someone who probably had enough money to buy Össur outright could not just say "lets get on with it". Was that really so difficult to do or was I being too unreasonable? In my opinion, surely if you promised someone like Maria something you would do everything in your power to fulfill those promises, regardless of costs, especially if you were hugely wealthy. And I also wondered whether they had any idea of what being disabled is like in a country like Russia. I looked at Heather's website in detail and noticed that apparently they worked in all sorts of third world countries, and yet they asked what was the possibility of Maria flying to St Petersburg to meet Heather? Did she expect a girl on a wooden platform to make her way to the airport, buy a ticket, get on a plane, fly to St Petersburg, get off the plane the other end and make her way to where Heather was staying, and then get back to Moscow again? I was absolutely astonished that Sonya could even ask such a question, but decided to hide my thoughts and feelings and reply.

From: Robin Barratt robinbarratt@yahoo.com
Date: Fri, 28 May 2004 03:08
To: Sonya Mills sonya@heathermillsmccartney.com
Subject: Re: FW: Maria

Hi Sonya

You should have got (Jamie's) report, as we got ours almost two weeks ago!!! We were waiting for you and Heather to read it and get back to us!!! We shall copy ours and post it to you ASAP.

Although she would love to, it would be impossible for Maria to get to St Petersburg on her own and we simply don't have the resources to fly Inna to Moscow and then to fly / train onto St Petersburg with Maria stay somewhere etc. But we do hope to meet you guys one day.

Call us if you need to, we are in most of today.

Regards as always

Robin

Jamie also replied answering Sonya's questions (edited excluding the original questions)

"Dear Sonya, I'm not familiar with the Russian American Medical Centre in Moscow and I don't know the standard of their prosthetics. I have suggested that if this cooperation goes ahead I would work with the prosthetic team in this facility to make sure the best outcome is provided to Maria. We have to think about prosthetic service after we leave. It's important that the local prosthetist is more than capable to carry out minor adjustments and when the time comes be able to produce good new sockets. By working with the local team I hope to educate them as we work, so they can possibly support Maria and the remainder of their patients better in the future. I'll also build a relationship so that we can stay in touch in the future to be able to answer any questions they may have.

It's common in many Russian prosthetic clinics for the limb user to stay as an in patient while the prosthesis is being manufactured. This is normal in many cities, but again I'm not sure about this Russian American Medical Centre.

Gait and strength training from a physio is essential if Maria is to get the best from her limbs. Unfortunately gait training is very poor in Russia and in many cases the prosthetist carries this out which is not ideal. I asked the same question to Robin on my return. I'm working with our local colleagues in Moscow at the moment to try and find the best solution for this. I agree that this is one of the most important aspects of prosthetic teamwork. As a last resort if all else fails we may have the opportunity to provide physio support. This may also be used as an educational session for local physios.

I am hoping to travel to Russia in June/July and would like to arrange a visit to the Russian American Family Medical Centre to meet the local prosthetic team. I will then have a better idea of their level of expertise.

I am now based in the UK in Croxley Green, Hertfordshire. I am a qualified prosthetist (and transtibial amputee). I left the military and came into the profession after a motor cycle accident a couple of months before Heather's accident. After University I worked in RNOH Stanmore before moving over to Iceland to work for Össur at their head office for a couple of years in their research and development department. I moved back to the UK during the end of last year and my current position is with the international markets department of Össur. My job is to travel and work with local prosthetists (and multidisciplinary teams) in many countries around the world. I work closely with prosthetists and their patients to try and introduce more up to date procedures that will increase comfort and mobility rather than some of the dated procedures they currently use. My work is not only focused on Össur products, and the majority of my time is spent improving comfort and function of the limb users I work with. I travel approximately half to two thirds of the month and when not on the road I work from home.

As you'll see from my report I have suggested a possible prescription that I think will be the best solution for Maria. It's common in Russia for transfemoral amputation to be carried out high with little residual limb remaining. As I'm sure Heather is aware Össur was born as a silicone company and offer a range of silicone liners.

There is a silicone liner that has been designed especially for transfemoral limbs that I'm using very successfully in Russia within the hospitals that I visit. These work well with the short limbs and the huge bonus is that no straps are required on the outside of the limbs so that when used with a good socket design a very comfortable, functional sockets can be produced that is aesthetic and cannot be seen through clothing. These liners work on a similar principle to those provided by Dorset Orthopaedic. The main difference is that these are not custom made and are selected according to the type of silicone required and the correct sizing. This offers a benefit in this case as new liner can be provided "off the shelf" and used in the same sockets when the time comes without new casts being required.

Maria is a very pretty young lady and my suggested prescription keeps this in mind. No straps will be required. The knees are quiet and safe and the feet allow Maria to wear different types of shoes with varying heel heights. She will be able to adjust these to whatever shoes she wants to wear rather than have to choose shoes that are most suited for her limbs.

I work regularly with bilateral transfemoral amputees who walk on two limbs. These are mainly young motivated people following trauma and if the will is there, these people can walk and walk well.

Jamie"

Sonya must have spoken to Heather as a few days later we heard from her informing us that Heather was hoping to fly to Moscow on the 20th June and they were a bit concerned that Heather would not be able to communicate with Maria. She asked if anyone would be able to be in Moscow on that date to meet Heather and translate for Maria.

Aside from everything it was great to hear that Heather was planning to go to Moscow and that she wanted to meet Maria. It would be simply amazing for a girl begging on the streets of Moscow to meet Heather Mills-McCartney. It was something that I could never have predicted, let alone Maria. Was this really going to happen? Was Heather really going to fly to Moscow and see Maria? It was impossible to believe.

We had arranged to meet Jamie in central London on the 7th June, outside Covent Garden underground station. I was really looking forward to meeting him. He had done so much for us already, more than we could have imagined, and he was truly dedicated to Maria. Having his backing and commitment meant we also had the backing and commitment of Össur and Össur had the funds to make some really good legs for Maria. She would be walking soon and that was wonderful.

Inna immediately recognised Jamie leaning against a wall opposite the entrance and rushed over to greet him. I was really pleased to finally meet him, and honoured, and warmly shook his hand. He said he only had about an hour spare and so we quickly walked to a café in Covent Garden, found an outside table in the sun and ordered three coffees. We sat chatting for a while and he told us of the plans Össur had for Maria and the possible dates for the final fitting. Jamie told us that, in his own time, he would personally go to Moscow and spend a week with Maria. All he asked for were expenses, which we were sure Heather would cover. He said he only needed a bed, nothing special as most of the time he would be at the clinic. Again that would keep the costs low as hotels in Moscow are generally quite expensive. We assured him that, despite the few difficulties we had had with Heather's office, she had promised us her total support. At that time Jamie didn't have a specific date when he could fly to Moscow but he said it would probably be early August. Two months wasn't long, we had waited almost a year and Maria had waited a lifetime, so we could all wait another couple of months. We finished our coffees and, just as Jamie got up to leave, my phone rang. I quickly said goodbye to Jamie and answered my call. It was Sonya. I sat down and as I watched Jamie walk back towards the underground, Sonya told me that they had decided they were not going continue with this project and that, for the money they would be spending on providing Maria with the cosmesis for her legs, the charity could help a lot more children in other countries. I tried and tried to explain to Sonya that Heather had promised, off her own back and not via her charity, that she would help, but Sonya kept saying that it wasn't the case, that Heather had now decided she wasn't going to spend any money on Maria. Maria would have to settle with the legs from Össur without any silicone covering and it is doubtful whether any of the other expenses will be met by Heather either – they will let us know about that in due course.

Inna and I sat there shocked. We were so upset. Five minutes earlier we were talking to Jamie and felt over the moon and so positive about everything, and now we were told that none of it was going to happen because, for some reason, Heather had now changed her mind. I had spoken to Heather a few times and each and every time I spoke to her she complained and moaned about the press and the media and how awful they all are to her, and then she suddenly turns round and decides not to fulfill a promise she had faithfully made to someone so much less fortunate than herself. Heather spent time on the streets, Heather lost the lower part of her leg – she had been through a lot of what Maria had been through and now she had turned round and taken away the hope of a woman she had given hope to. How could someone so wealthy, so much in the public light, someone who says she is so pre-occupied with helping others all of a sudden turn round and decide on such an appalling cruel thing. How could someone that says she really does care do something so uncaring and unkind? Her and her husband Paul McCartney were said to be worth over eight hundred million pounds so why couldn't Heather just do what she promised she would? Up to that time Heather had done not a single thing for Maria, even though she promised she would. Up to that time Heather had not spent one penny – she had just gone back on all the promises she made. As soon as we got home we wrote an e-mail to her, copying it to the Directors at Össur. I was angry and wanted them to see what Heather had done.

Date: Mon, 7 Jun 2004 14:41
From: "Robin Barratt" robinbarratt@yahoo.com
Subject: Re: Maria and conversation with Sonya this morning
To: "Sonya Mills" sonya@heathermillsmccartney.com,
heather@heathermillsmccartney.com
CC: "Össur" sarnarsdottir@Össur.com, "Jamie Gillespie" jgillespie@Össur.com

Dear Heather
Following my conversation with Sonya this morning, literally just a few minutes after we had a meeting with Jamie from Össur, I feel I have to discuss the topics of the conversation with Sonya in detail as she notified us that you will definitely not pay for the cosmesis and it is now questionable as to whether you are going to fund this project at all.

Maria is in the same position as you were many years ago,

except she still wheels herself around on a wooden board and still begs on the streets to provide for her son. After all this time and planning, we cannot ask Maria to wear skeleton legs, but Sonya said she will have to.

When you first called us, after receiving our letter, you stressed that you will fund this project independent from your charities. We also confirmed this with you a second time just before we flew out to meet Maria, as we certainly did not want to promise Maria anything we couldn't fulfill. On both occasions you categorically confirmed your commitment and promise to get Maria new legs. Your words to us were that you will get her the best legs possible as you said by yourself that if she had poor uncomfortable legs she would never use them. These were your words.

Initially we discussed bringing Maria to the UK for a couple of weeks where she would have her legs fitted in the Dorset clinic, but we eventually decided that it would be much easier for Maria to have her legs fitted in Moscow rather than making the journey to the UK. You even instructed us to look for suitable facilities.

As you know I managed to get a commitment from Össur to actually supply the legs.

Now we have been told that you will not in fact pay for the cosmesis and it is doubtful you will pay for her fitting, medical expenses etc. Your definite promise and commitment to Maria has changed completely. Össur have agreed to provide the limbs, Jamie has agreed to work with Maria in Moscow for a week without payment and we have spent our own time and money flying to Moscow to take Maria for her first examination. We have all done this without question, hesitation or doubt and regardless of whether she did or did not have limbs given to her in the past. This is irrelevant but it is now your reason for not helping.

We have promised Maria everything because you have promised this to us. Maria is so looking forward to starting a new life because you promised us, and Össur, and Jamie that you will fund this project yourself. Now what do we tell her, that you have changed your mind. Don't you think this girl has had enough trauma and hardship in her life?

From the very beginning, you asked us that you did not want any publicity over this and throughout we have respected your wishes. This has obviously prevented us from raising as much money as we could have done. We were also intending to make a wonderful documentary on Maria and her life and the help your had promised to give, which would have done so much good for both your charity and for Maria. But again you didn't want to be involved and so we abandoned this idea. Also we never once called and disturbed you after our initial discussions, trusting your kind intentions. We have respected every one of your wishes as we genuinely believed you would personally help Maria and honor your promise.

Now Sonya says it is doubtful you will.

So everyone involved – Össur, Jamie, ourselves and of course Maria and her son must now just sit and wait until you might, or might not decide to help. And if you don't, what happens? Has everyone's kindness gone to waste and what do we tell Maria?

This is fundamentally wrong, unfair and unkind. You cannot make false promises to someone in the situation like Maria's.

Russia is not like England and she will never have an opportunity to obtain good legs and thus change her life without our help.

Is it that impossible for you to commit yourself regardless of the cost? The costs won't be excessive anyway. We will negotiate good rates with the clinic in Moscow, and you have good contacts for the cosmesis in the UK.

We understand you have many commitments and obligations, but it was you that called us, you that made these promises to us and to Maria.

We have copied this e-mail to everyone involved in helping Maria as they should all have the right to know and understand the situation.

As you know I am a writer and like you have travelled the world and seen many sad stories. Is this going to be another?

We all await your reply.

Three days later she telephoned me. She was so angry, almost shouting at me down the phone. How could I write such a letter she yelled? She said it was all a big misunderstanding, and that she was indeed going to help as she had originally promised. I have to ask myself how such a call from Sonya was a "misunderstanding"? I am sure Sonya didn't just decide to make up the story and call us that afternoon, thinking that might be a good thing to do. Throughout all our dealings with Heather there has been so called "misunderstanding" after "misunderstanding." To be honest I was sick of it all but I remained polite and civil as I still wanted Heather to help and I was still determined that Heather would fulfill the promises she made to Maria. But above all Inna and I still desperately wanted Maria to walk.

During that heated and awkward conversation Heather confirmed that she would be flying to Moscow from St Petersburg, where Paul McCartney was playing in concert, to meet Maria. A couple of days later I wrote back to Heather and I sent Sonya the contact and address details of Maria's hostel.

Date: Sun, 13 Jun 2004 14:29
From: "Robin Barratt" robinbarratt@yahoo.com
Subject: Maria
To: heather@heathermillsmccartney.com
CC: sarnarsdottir@Össur.com, jgillespie@Össur.com,
irichter@Össur.com, "Sonya Mills"
sonya@heathermillsmccartney.com

Dear Heather
Thanks for your call on Thursday. We completely understand you help many people all over the world, and yet we can only help the one, but it was really good to speak to you and to know that you are indeed committed to Maria and the support and help she will need once her legs have been fitted.

We have spoken to Maria and she is looking forward to meeting you next Saturday. It is great that you will fly from St Petersburg to see her. My wife Inna will be with Maria waiting for you at the hostel next week. I believe you have already arranged the time and that you have the address. The building where Maria lives is quite big with over 1000 rooms, so please make sure you call Inna once you arrive as you may easily get lost. There are two buildings with four entrances and Maria lives in the second.

Jamie will be visiting Moscow in July to make arrangements with the clinic, and in August he will then go over again to make and fit her legs.

Thanks again, please feel free to call us at anytime. Our home number and my mobile is below, Inna's Moscow number again is (From Russia) XXXXXXXXX. If at any stage you cannot get hold of Inna please call me and I will contact her myself.

Regards

Robin

Heather had planned to meet Maria in Moscow on Saturday 19th June. Both Heather and Maria needed Inna there, Inna could not only translate but she was the only person that Maria really trusted. We told Heather that we couldn't afford the flight for Inna, we were living hand by mouth and simply didn't even have three hundred pounds needed for the return flight. Heather said that if we could pay by credit card she would reimburse Inna when they met that Saturday. But we didn't have a credit card. I had a debit card but there weren't enough funds in my bank to cover the cost. I called my mother and asked if she could lend us the money and we'll give it back to her on Monday when Inna got home. She said no. We didn't know many people in Norwich and, apart from my mother who refused to help, we were stuck. Inna suggested we ask Jim, who led the Russian group. Inna taught Russian to them every Tuesday and they had already donated money to Maria. We were a little embarrassed but he kindly agreed and Inna arranged to meet Jim at the travel agents where they bought a ticket to Moscow.

Inna flew to Moscow Friday afternoon. We had had so many disappointments we fully expected Heather not to turn up. We would then have to explain this to Maria as well as having to find the money to pay Jim back. Inna tried calling Heather on the Friday evening before they were due to meet, but left a couple of messages on her voice mail as she couldn't get through. She also tried calling that morning, but again no reply.

Inna made her way over to the hostel, still not knowing whether or not Heather was going to come. Inna arrived at the hostel at about eleven am and called Maria from the lobby. Maria was upstairs getting ready and a few minutes later came down to meet Inna. They hugged and kissed and Inna gave her some toys for her son and a couple of gifts for her. And then suddenly Heather called, she was in Moscow and on her way from the airport!! Nervously Maria and Inna went back up to her room and waited for Heather to arrive. Inna had bought a nice card for Maria to give to Heather. Maria sat on the bed and wrote a message to Heather, thanking her for her help and her kindness. Heather called Inna again, she was in the lobby. Inna and Maria fussed around, quickly tidying up a little. Heather called again – where were they, she was waiting. As Inna rushed down to meet them, Heather called for the third time. "Coming" Inna called as she entered the lobby. Inna felt nervous too, but immediately recognised Heather, immaculately dressed and looking beautiful, yet a little out of place standing in a run-down Moscow hostel lobby. She was with her female bodyguard and Sofia, who was going to help translate. As they all went upstairs Inna kept looking at Heather's legs, wondering which one had been amputated. It was impossible to tell.

Maria timidly opened the door to her room and nervously greeted Heather. She wasn't sure what to say, but Heather took control and greeted her warmly and affectionately. Heather sat on the chair opposite Maria, Heather's bodyguard and Sofia sat on the bed and Inna stood awkwardly next to Maria, holding her hand. There was little space in Maria's room and it seemed a little cramped and everyone felt a little uncomfortable.

"Why don't you sit yourself down over there," Heather told Inna. She sat down against the wall near to Maria. Heather looked at Maria and smiled.

"Have you read my book?" she asked Inna.

"No," Inna replied, she didn't know Heather had written a book.

"Well you should do," Heather said. Heather started to tell Maria her story. When she was five her mother had a terrible car accident when she almost lost her leg. She spent almost twelve months in hospital during which Heather and her sister lived in a children's home. Heather grew up in a difficult home with an abusive father who frequently used violence on Heather, her sister Fiona and her mother. Unable to take the beatings and torments her mother eventually moved out, leaving her children with their father. He would frequently force Heather and Fiona to steal clothes and food as they could rarely afford to buy things themselves. Heather's father was eventually sent to prison for fraud and Heather and Fiona then went to live with their mother. Heather left home at around fifteen years old as she couldn't get on with her new stepfather. She lived on the streets of London for a while. She was spotted after a friend sent her photograph off to a beauty contest. She eventually became a model and did a range of catwalk and advertising campaigns for numerous reputable companies. In 1993, when Heather was just twenty five years old and just as she was developing her career as a model, she had a horrific accident. A police motorcyclist, on his way to what turned out to be a false alarm, collided with her, sending her somersaulting in the air and almost severing her leg. She also suffered crushed ribs, a punctured lung, and multiple fractures of the pelvis. As she slowly recovered she approached various magazines and newspapers and eventually sold her story from the hospital bed. Her first artificial leg was horrible, extremely uncomfortable and almost impossible to wear. As time passed she started a campaign for better prosthetics for amputees.

Maria listened as Inna translated. There seemed to be lots of parallels between Maria's life and Heather's and Inna had the impression that Heather knew and understood this. They both lived in abusive and unstable homes, they both had horrific accidents and they both had lived on the streets. Heather spoke to Maria about her being an ambassador for other disabled in Russia. She could see in Maria a strength of character and personality and felt Maria was strong enough to lobby for change and fight for the rights of other disabled. Heather told Maria that she was also willing to financially sponsor Maria for two or three months while she gets off the streets and looks for work. They talked about Heather's contacts in Moscow and that she might be able to help Maria find a job, and she said she would even pay Maria while she trains. During all this time Maria continued to stare at Heather's leg. Like Inna, she also couldn't tell which leg was real and which was false. Heather asked Maria if she minded if her bodyguard filmed the rest of their meeting. She would then present the film to the Dorset clinic and hopefully get a discount on the cosmesis covering she had promised to provide for Maria's legs once they had been fitted. Heather told Maria that she helped design the cosmesis covering, and then she took off her leg and handed it over to Maria. Maria sat with it on her lap, amazed and enthralled at its detail and intricacy.

Maria looked up at Heather and said "I want the same."
Heather replied "You'll have the same."

Heather took out a picture of Beatrice, Heather's
daughter, and handed it to Maria. She told Maria how this
was the first time Heather had left her daughter alone, and
that her husband, Sir Paul McCartney is currently looking
after her. Maria didn't know what "Sir" meant, but of
course she knew who Paul McCartney was. Heather
remarked upon Maria's hair, saying how lovely it was.
Maria and Inna saw a certain genuine understanding and
compassion in Heather.

Heather said that they had to go soon, as they had a flight
to catch back to St Petersburg. She suggested they take some
pictures of her and Maria as maybe Maria could sell them to
the Russian press and make a little money. Inna informed
Heather that although it initially sounds a good idea, copy-
right laws in Russia are almost non-existent and the pictures
would quickly be used without any permission being granted
and almost certainly without any payment to Maria. And a
girl on the streets could do little about it. But they took some
pictures for their own records and Heather suggested they go
downstairs for something quick to eat.

The typically Russian café downstairs wasn't particularly
busy and they all sat around a small, slightly unsteady table
being stared at by other Russians sitting nearby. As they came
to order, Inna quickly found out that Heather was vegetarian
and that there was only the one dish on the already basic
menu that could be vaguely classed as vegetarian. As they sat
and ate and chatted a little more, Maria said she would one
day like to wear high heels. Heather told Maria about wearing
high heels and that she must always need to know the exact
height of the heels of shoes she buys as this affects the alignment of her leg. Whenever she goes shopping she brings with
her a ruler and measures every shoe she considers buying.

It was time to go and, as they said their goodbyes, Maria

gave Heather the card and Heather gave Maria an envelope with money and her address back in the UK. She also turned to Inna and, to Inna's surprise, handed her an envelope with the money for her flight. Inna walked with them to the car as Maria waited in the hotel lobby doorway, watching them leave and waving goodbye.

Inna sat with Maria in the café for an hour or so after Heather had left, chatting about the many things only women find to chat about. Maria had found a friend in Inna.

After Heather's meeting with Maria we were really happy that things had got back on track and that everything was panning out perfectly. Heather had now met Maria and we felt sure that everything was now going to go ahead as planned without any further "misunderstanding" or problems. Jamie had also met Maria and confirmed that new limbs could be fitted. I wrote an e-mail to Jamie telling him of the meeting and everything that had happened and that once we had Maria off that platform and walking we could go onto help others like Maria. Jamie replied.

To: "Robin Barratt" robinbarratt@yahoo.com
CC: irichter@Össur.com, "Össur" sarnarsdottir@Össur.com
Subject: Re: Maria
From: jgillespie@Össur.com
Date: Sun, 27 Jun 2004 20:55

Hi Robin,
Thanks for the update.
I'm so glad things went well last weekend and especially glad that Heather could find the time to visit Maria at her home.

I'm also happy that this will lead onto bigger and better things. We have this one opportunity to help Maria get back on her feet comfortably but as we both know there are many more, less fortunate people in Russia who are not in this fortunate position that Maria is in.

Your contacts and efforts with the media will help a great deal to show Russia (and the world) that with modern prosthetic technology, education in socket design and effective cosmesis there is no reason in this day and age that people cannot be integrated back into society with a prosthetic limb(s). Let's show the world what we can do!

Please also pass on my sincere thanks to Heather for continuing her support with this project. I'm a realistic person and of course money does play a part in this team support that is being provided to Maria. The prosthetic industry in Russia does have money, and I can clearly see this from my visits to rehabilitation centers in Russia. This work has two main goals. Firstly we'll get Maria walking with highly functional and cosmetic looking prosthesis, and secondly we will open the eyes of Russian prosthetists and prosthetic budget holders and show them that excellent clinical outcome is financially achievable with their funding.

I leave for the US tomorrow for a week and then immediately following this I travel to China to help prepare their athletes for the Para-Olympic games in the summer. My trip to Russia in July is looking very very difficult. As we discussed the purpose of this trip was to carry out a 'recce' in preparation for the prosthetic work for Maria in August. It now seems that I may have to do this remotely which is not a problem. I have a prosthetic workshop that I can use in Moscow to carry out the manufacture of the sockets and assembly of the prosthesis. Fittings will be carried out at the Russian American Medical Centre that you have found and finally the cosmesis will be added in the UK.

I'm suggesting that I will fly to Russia on the 22nd of August for work to commence on the 23rd. I'll then work closely with Maria for the week before flying back to the UK the following weekend. How does this sound? I'm aware that everyone is keen to see this move forward and I'm also looking forward to this work both on a personal level and also a professional level, but this is the earliest I'm free for one week's work. Can you please see if these dates fit with everyone involved?

For both trips in July I will have my mobile phone with me so please call me if need be. As soon as I hear from you regarding dates I'll put the wheels in motion.

One final point regarding media coverage. The Iceross silicone liners we will be using as an interface between Maria's legs and the prosthetic sockets are made in Iceland, and both the knees and feet that we'll use are made in one of our manufacturing facilities in the US. I will cast Maria with plaster of paris-bandage and then modify the plaster model of Maria's legs in Moscow. I will also manufacture the prosthetic sockets and assemble and fit the prosthesis in Moscow. By the end of my week in Moscow Maria will be walking comfortably on two prosthesis without cosmetic covers. The covers will be added in the UK and then final fitting carried out in Moscow.

Hope this helps with the media support from your end.

I'll look forward to hearing from you.

Cheers

Jamie Gillespie

We now had confirmed dates from Jamie as to when he could manage to get back to Moscow and finally fit Maria's new legs. Things were now progressing quicker than we had anticipated, in only seven months Össur had assessed Maria and her needs and put into motion a plan to finally get her walking. We now had to arrange everything else including Jamie's accommodation and flights. We knew that he wasn't at all fussed as to where he would stay, he just needed somewhere to crash at the end of the day. We wanted to keep costs as low as possible for Heather and so asked everyone we knew for suggestions. A couple of our friends in Moscow suggested cheap hotels, but they were Russian and we didn't really want Jamie staying in a typically Russian hotel. We wouldn't feel that he and all the expensive components he would be taking with him were safe. We wrote to Heather explaining things so far.

Date: Mon, 26 Jul 2004 06:03
From: "Robin Barratt" robinbarratt@yahoo.com
Subject: From ROBIN AND INNA – Re Maria / MOSCOW
To: "Heather" heather@heathermillsmccartney.com
CC: sonya@heathermillsmccartney.com

Hi Heather,
Hope you are well. We have just spoken to Jamie who plans to go to Moscow on the 22nd August to fit Maria's legs. Below is a letter that he has written to the clinic in Moscow asking for their help. Although Inna has just started a full-time job, she will try to fly her to Moscow to be there with Maria and Jamie for that week.

Jamie is donating a week of his time but we will have to find him basic accommodation / food etc, and pay for the medical centre, although, to keep costs down, Maria said she will try and stay there as least time as possible. We will get the costs on this as soon as we can and call you.

We know you are really busy but if possible we would like to meet up again in the next couple of weeks and sort everything out. Maria wants to help others and fight for the rights of the less able in Russia as you have. After meeting her she sees you as a role model and looks forward to her future – for the first time in her life. We also hope to one day help her and others like her.

Hope you get this e-mail and look forward to talking again soon. Please feel free to contact Jamie at anytime – his details are below.
Kindest regards as always
Inna and Robin

Jamie already made contacts in Moscow and found a Russian prosthetic company that he could possibly work with. They had good facilities and a workshop. He had made contact with a man named Andrey, one of the managers, and had written to him asking for their assistance.

We then heard from Heather. She seemed pleased that everything was moving forward and gave us her new contact telephone number, just in case we needed anything. She said she was really busy with Iraqi amputees but we should let her know costs as soon as we could and she would make sure she gets the money to us. This was great news.

A few days later Andrey replied to Jamie confirming that they would indeed be willing to help. Their company would allocate their own time and their own expenses in order to work with Jamie, Össur and Maria. This was more great news as firstly Jamie now had a confirmed workshop as it would have been quite difficult and time consuming trying to find somewhere suitable and secondly, it would now save Heather even more money as she would not have to pay for the use of a workshop either.

Even though she was enormously wealthy, we always considered Heather and always tried to save money as and when we could. We thought that the more we saved the more willing she would be to pay for the other things that we needed, such as the clinic for Maria to stay in while she was being fitted, her medical expenses, Jamie's, Inna's and Maria's expenses etc. We spoke to her on the 4th August when she yet again confirmed everything she had written a few days earlier – promising she would get any money we needed to us.

We asked Heather to send us one thousand pounds to book Jamie's flight, find accommodation and help with other daily costs such as food, travel backwards and forwards to the clinic and workshop etc. We would also have to pay for Maria's medical expenses. We would provide Heather with receipts for everything. She refused. Heather refused to send us any money whatsoever. She said, so that there would be no confusion, she would pay for Inna's flight and that the price should be agreed in advance and paid direct to the airline. She said she had had too many experiences (of precisely what, we weren't sure) with too many people to personally fund with no money coming in. She said she would pay for Maria's costs at the clinic, direct to the clinic which must also be agreed in advance. She said that the clinic should know their costs, but we had already e-mailed her details and the costs of accommodation and it would be very difficult to have given Heather precise costs of the treatment and physiotherapy in advance until the Medical Centre had properly assessed Maria. She told us she would not pay for any other unnecessary costs and ended by saying she hoped that we were pleased with what she had done for us so far.

From her initial promises that she would do everything to get Maria walking again, Heather was now not going to pay for Jamie's flight, his accommodation or food as well as expenses for Jamie, Inna and Maria during their stay in Moscow. These costs she now considered unnecessary. All she had done for us up to that point was to pay for two flights and the only thing she had personally done for Maria was give her a very small amount of money. Maria was still begging, and she had the audacity to say that she hoped we were happy with all that she had done for us so far. Again Heather had caused us so many problems. How could we afford to pay for Jamie's flight, his accommodation and all the expenses? It was simply impossible. We were completely stuck. We didn't know what we were going to do. We were going to have to try and raise as much money as we could in following two weeks, but we just didn't know how. A couple of days later we heard from Sonya, saying that Heather would now pay for Jamie's flight, as apparently she now considered that as essential. But Jamie still ended up paying for the flight from his own pocket, he never sent her the receipt and they never again asked for it.

A few weeks earlier we had made contact with Tania Illingworth, based in London. She was Russian and ran a small charity for Russians. She promised to help us all she could. She wasn't at all wealthy but kindly sent a hundred pounds to help pay for Jamie's expenses and accommodation. She had also asked her brother to contact us. Her brother lived in Russia and knew of somewhere comfortable in central Moscow where Jamie could stay. He was close friends with Olga Nikolaevna Adamishina – wife of former Ambassador to Great Britain and Trustee of British Charity – Russian Arts Help. She spoke fluent English and had a spare room which she gladly agreed to let Jamie use for the duration of his stay. Inna called her from the UK a few days before she and Jamie was due to fly to Moscow and arranged everything. It was such short notice but Olga was so helpful and so kind. We promised Tania that we would give the hundred pounds to Olga as a thank you, but when we offered it to her she refused. Instead we gave it to her charity.

Apart from the problems Inna and I now had financing Jamie, everything was now more or less in place. Össur will be providing all the prosthetic components free of charge including the liners, knees and feet plus the connecting adapters. They will also provide the prosthetic service free of charge and Jamie's time in Moscow for that week. The use of the workshop will also be free in co-operation with Jamie's local business partner Andrey. Össur will also cover the cost of prosthetic materials used for the prostheses – all the materials used to produce the sockets and check sockets that are used as a half way stage to confirm the comfortable fitting of the definitive sockets. Jamie's Moscow contact had also agreed to work with Maria free of charge on an ongoing basis after the initial fitting, as it is common for the prosthetic knee settings to need adjusting slightly to allow for the stiffness of the foam and skin. And lastly we had found free accommodation. A few days before Inna was due to fly, Sonya sent her flight tickets.

Inna called Maria a few days before she was due to leave just to make sure everything was fine. Unusually she managed to get through the first time, but strangely Maria had seemed to have changed – she was not the Maria Inna knew and had spoken to many times before, or the Maria she had seen with Heather and with Jamie. She sounded very unhappy. Somehow she had it in her mind that there was no way Jamie could do anything for her in just one week. The Russians had taken months, if not years to provide her with limbs that were so uncomfortable and so horrible that she never wore them, so what could Jamie do in just one week. According to Maria, nothing. She had it in her mind that the legs Jamie was going to fit were going to be just as awful and she didn't want them, simple. Inna asked her how she knew what they were going to be like when she hadn't even seen them. Apparently she had met Andrey at his Moscow office a week earlier as Jamie asked him to measure her limbs again for the final fitting. Andrey had shown Maria some components, but the components he had shown her were not the components Jamie was bringing with him and this sometimes stubborn, tough, streetwise woman had it in her mind that they were exactly the ones that she will be having and Inna was finding it impossible to get her to change her mind. She also said she didn't want to stay in the clinic. She hated the thought of staying there alone. Inna didn't really know what to say and asked her to please wait and not to make any decisions until they met and she can see everything for herself. Maria sounded strange and certainly not her usual optimistic, positive self. What had really happened to change her mind? What had been said to her? Had anyone influenced her? It was hard to tell on the telephone, but when Inna hung up she was worried that, after everything that had happened so far, things were not going to work out as planned.

On Friday the 20th August 2004 Inna flew to Moscow and was met at the airport by her parents. Jamie was due to arrive on Sunday and so, before what was going to be an extremely exhausting and traumatic week, Inna spent a nice relaxing day at home with her family. They all had dinner together, drank a little wine, made various toasts and generally had a nice time.

On Sunday Inna woke up early as she had to make her way from Zelenograd, about thirty miles north of Moscow, to Domodedovo airport about ten miles south of Moscow. She had to take the minibus from Zelenograd to Rechnoy Vokzal Metro – at the very end of the Green Metro line. She then had to catch a Metro to Paveletsky railway station at Metro Paveletskaya, on the circle line and from Paveletsky she had to take a train to the airport. It was a long, hot, uncomfortable three hour journey.

She got there in plenty of time and waited for Jamie's flight to arrive. It didn't take him long to get through passport control and customs, Domodedovo airport is so much better, a lot more modern and much more efficient that Sheremetyevo, which was one of the reasons British Airways had moved there a couple of years previously. More and more western airlines are moving to Domodedovo as it is as modern as any other smaller International airport and has a distinctive European feeling and service, which is totally opposite to the typically awful Russian service you get at Sheremetyevo.

Inna hugged Jamie as he walked through the arrivals gate. Everything seemed a little unreal. Was Jamie was really finally arriving to complete something Inna and I had been planning for almost two years? From an initial conversation outside a grubby Metro here was Jamie in Moscow with a satchel full of components which could, quite possibly, change a person's life forever. Sitting in my little apartment in Norwich wondering about the coming week, I thought about Jamie and how many countries he had walked into with bags full of components and how wonderful he must feel being able to help so many. After losing his leg and also suffering terribly, he now travels around the world lecturing and consulting and helping hundreds and hundreds of people change their lives. By his own admission and time and time again he says he wouldn't change a thing.

Inna and Jamie caught the train back into Moscow and made their way to the apartment in which we had arranged for him to stay. Olga was still at her dacha (country house) but would be returning sometime during the week. She had spoken to Inna the day before and arranged to leave the keys with a neighbour. Sometimes people in Moscow can be so harsh and unkind and unhelpful, but sometimes they can be the complete opposite and do so much more than most people would ever think about doing in the UK. Olga hadn't met Inna or Jamie, Inna had only had a couple of conversations with her on the telephone and yet she agreed to let Jamie stay without any question or comment, even entrusting the keys to a neighbour. I don't know many people in England that would be willing do this. The neighbour showed them around; Jamie's room, the bathroom, the kitchen and where the tea and coffee was kept. He then bade them farewell, saying if they needed anything else just call, and left them the keys.

Inna called Olga again to confirm they had arrived and settled and thanked her once again for all her help and everything she had done. Olga told Inna to make sure that

Jamie was comfortable and that her son would be popping by shortly to ensure everything was all right. She will be back from the country in a couple of days.

While Inna made some tea and looked at the photographs on Olga's sideboard of Olga sitting with Princess Diana, with the Queen and Russian government officials, Jamie sorted his things and freshened up.

That Sunday evening they had arranged to meet Andrey at a local café to plan the week ahead. It was going to be a very busy week, and very hard work. Time was critically important – they would have so much to do, every day from early morning until late at night. It wasn't going to be easy, even more tiring for Inna who was going to have to travel from Zelenograd into Moscow and back. Andrey, Jamie and Inna met at "Moo Moo" on Arbat Street in the centre of the city. Once home of the Russian aristocracy and where Pushkin once lived, Arbat is probably *the* tourist street of Moscow. With its stalls and buskers, peddlers and artists, lines of restaurants and souvenir shops it stretched from Metro Arbatskaya at the junction of Nikitskiy Boulevard to McDonald's at Smolenskaya. On a warm summer evening Arbat is always full with Russians and foreigners alike strolling slowly along its route, browsing, eating ice-cream, and stopping occasionally to listen to the buskers or watch the street theatre.

Jamie told Inna that Andrey was one of the best prosthetists in Moscow and again Inna was surprised with how young he was. She expected an expert in his field to have been a lot older, but, like Jamie he was also in his late twenties or early thirties. They sat and discussed the week ahead. Inna told Jamie about the conversation she had had with Maria a few days earlier. The plan was, as long as everything was back to normal with Maria, and they would only know that once they met her the following morning, that Maria would stay at the Russian American

Family Medical Center for a week while Jamie and Andrey went backwards and forwards to the workshop. Inna had called the Clinic the day before and confirmed that they would be arriving at ten o'clock that following Monday morning. She had spoken to them about the project and their requirements and the doctor in charge confirmed that everything would be fine and was looking forward to meeting them all.

Inna called Maria and yet again she seemed odd, unusual, not her normal self. She reluctantly arranged to meet Andrey at nine in the morning. He would pick her up from the train station and take her over to the clinic where they would meet Inna and Jamie. Maria no longer lived at the hostel, she moved out shortly after she had met Heather. The hostel owners could no longer continue to offer Maria a discount on the room. Through their initial kindheartedness they had only charged her fifty roubles a night for the whole time she had been living there, but they now asked for four times that amount. Rumour might have circulated that Maria knew some wealthy foreigners and could now perhaps afford to pay more, but Maria simply could not afford it and so found a room in the village of Lunevo about fifteen miles from Moscow. Sasha and Irina, whom she stayed with when she first escaped the gypsies, lived in the next village.

What was wrong with Maria and why was she behaving in the way that she was? She wasn't the Maria that everyone had got to know and love, she wasn't the optimistic Maria, the Maria that wanted to get off the streets. Was this all going to fall apart at the very last minute? Something was really wrong and the following day was going to decide what eventually was going to happen to everyone, and everything.

No one slept particularly well that night. Inna escorted Jamie back to the apartment and then caught the late Metro and bus back to Zelenograd. It took her almost two hours to get home, and, even though she was exhausted and had to be up extra early the next day to get back into Moscow in enough time to meet Jamie and get over to the Clinic, couldn't sleep well either, tossing and turning and thinking about Maria. She understood that there was a reason, there must be as nobody changes that quickly and that dramatically without a reason. It was now completely possible that, because of Maria's bizarre new attitude and mind-set, everything will be called off and everyone would return to England and Maria would continue with her life on the streets and her rickety wooden platform. She felt sad for Maria because she knew that her life could ultimately change if only she opened her eyes and trusted the people around her that were trying to make it happen. Inna lay on her bed looking up at the ceiling wondering if it was all in vain, did Maria really want what we thought she wanted or was it just us, fooling ourselves, being just another couple of "do-gooders." Was it just us that wanted Maria to walk again? Had everything been arranged and planned just because we thought that it was what Maria wanted and not what she wanted herself? Or did she really want to walk comfortably again? Did she really want a new life?

The next morning Jamie and Inna were initially very impressed with the clinic. Jamie had seen many typically Russian clinics and this was certainly nothing like any of them. Clean, efficient looking, modern, from the downstairs reception area it looked be a good place for Maria to stay. Inna called the doctor in charge, whom she had already spoken to and had arranged everything. He was unavailable. She called him again, and again he was unavailable. They made their way into the lobby and spoke to the receptionist. She knew nothing of their visit and refused them passes. They waited in the lobby not knowing what to do or where to go, and finally, on the third attempt and almost a half an hour later than arranged, Inna managed to get hold of the doctor. He was stuck in traffic and would be a while longer but he told them to go to the Reception and ask for passes to the 8th floor to see Dr. Vladimir Kolesov. Finally they were issued passes but they were not allowed to take their cameras inside the building. Inna and Jamie explained the project and the probably publicity and the people involved but that made no difference. This was definitely the Russian side of the Russian American Family Medical Center. And it got worse.

Maria and Andrey arrived as Jamie and Inna disappeared upstairs to the 8th floor to try and sort everything out, Maria and Andrey were left waiting downstairs in the lobby. There was no one to meet Jamie and Inna as they got off the elevator and they wondered around for a short while looking for someone to talk to. Eventually they found the Head Nurse who was not aware of their visit – she had no idea who they were or what they were doing and anyway, she said, they had no spare rooms. The Nurse asked whether they had paid in advance. They said they hadn't paid anything but Inna had spoken to Doctor Kolesov and told him about Maria and the project, but he wasn't there and the nurse wanted to talk about money. Inna asked the nurse how much money she wanted as a deposit and the nurse told her they required two thousand five hundred dollars as an advance payment before anyone could stay even one night. Inna and Jamie were amazed, the deposit was more than they had originally quoted for the week. Inna asked for a discount, again explaining the project and the people involved. Absolutely no discounts, the nurse said. Inna then told the clinic that Heather Mills-McCartney would pay them direct but the nurse would only accept this if they received a fax confirming this from Heather herself, and Maria wouldn't be able to stay until they received it. What on earth were they going to do? Jamie had an Össur credit card and asked if that would be accepted, and of course the clinic confirmed that it would be acceptable. Just as Jamie sat down to sign the debit form, Inna told him to wait – they should go back downstairs and talk to Maria first.

When they got back downstairs Maria was really fed up, terribly unhappy and just wanted to go home. She certainly didn't want to stay at the clinic and have everyone stare at her, she didn't want new legs, she just wanted to go back to her old life, a life she knew and understood and could control and be in charge of.

They fell silent as the doctor finally arrived and extended his deepest apologies. The traffic in Moscow was getting worse by the day, he panted as he glanced around at everyone looking sullen and confused.

"Come, let's go upstairs," he said as he ushered everyone past the security guard and back into the elevator. They all went back up to 8th floor and into the conservatory garden.

Inna took the doctor to one side and quietly explained the situation and that they weren't yet sure whether Maria would be staying.

"Don't worry, just call me when you have made up your mind and I will make all the arrangements," he said "we can sort everything out once you have decided what you are going to do." He left.

The four of them sat together in the stillness of the garden. No matter how hard everyone tried to persuade Maria to the contrary, she absolutely believed that they could do nothing for her. According to Maria the legs that Jamie was going to make would be just like her Russian legs – uncomfortable and horrible. For Jamie this was the first patient he had ever had that was so negative and whom he had to try persuade to have the legs – usually it had been the other way round, his patients would beg Jamie for new legs. But Maria was an exception. She didn't want legs and told Jamie, Andrey and Inna that if she was given these legs she would never wear them, she would just throw them into the corner and forget about them. She said was also sick and tired with people making money on her – that they would benefit from any publicity yet she would still have to sit on the street corner with her hand out asking for money. Inna and Jamie denied that they were making money on Maria's misfortune, but agreed that yes, they would be getting publicity but in return Maria would be getting some of the best legs in the world. But, according to Maria we were like all the others that had promised her something but never had any intention of giving. No matter how hard Inna, Jamie and Andrey tried they simply could not change her mind. For some strange and incomprehensible reason her mind had been set and it seemed there was little anyone could do to change it.

He had just flown from the UK with thousands of pounds worth of components and now Jamie just didn't know what to do. While Maria sat depressed on her own, Jamie, Inna and Andrey went to have a private talk. It was apparent that Maria was not yet psychologically strong enough to have new legs – she simply couldn't yet cope with the enormous change to her life and to how she will be accepted by others around her.

Andrey left Jamie and Inna chatting and sat next to Maria, talking to her not as a foreign "do-gooder" – as she now seemed to perceived Inna and Jamie as being – but as a doctor, a Russian doctor and someone that she could identify with. They spoke quietly for a while, in whispered voices. Eventually Maria looked up at Andrey and, grudgingly, agreed to "give it a go."

But Jamie was still unconvinced. As a humanitarian he

desperately wanted Maria to walk. He had got to know and like Maria – he liked her strength and character and resilience and her optimistic attitude to the cruel life she had been given. But as a representative for Össur he couldn't waste the company's money by giving very expensive legs to someone that didn't want them and who might still end up throwing them unused into the corner, especially when there were so many others in the world that did desperately need them.

Jamie excused himself from the group and called me in England. As he explained the situation I sat silently listening to what had unfolded. I simply didn't know what to say. Finally, after listening to everything I said "Jamie, come home. If Maria doesn't want legs we can't give them to her. Come home." After a long silence he agreed and passed me over to Inna. I could hear in Inna's voice that she was really upset. She briefly told me the same things as Jamie had said, and I said to her the same thing as I had said to Jamie, come home. There was no point in staying, we have done what we can and we could do no more.

The line went silent and I suddenly felt very sad.

Jamie asked Inna to go and tell Maria that we could no longer help her. It had all abruptly ended. Maybe someday, he said, in the future, but not now. She quietly agreed and wondered over to the water container and poured herself a small cup full. She stood there thinking about what she was going to say and how she was going to say it. We had promised so much but had ended up giving so little. She felt sad for Maria. She knew that inside Maria was just a little girl lost in this big harsh world. She knew that Maria just needed guiding, she needed help in understanding that her life wasn't on the streets but with her son being a mother and a friend, but now she had to tell Maria that it was all over. Tears rolled down Inna's eyes. She just couldn't tell Maria, she couldn't do it, not now, not after everyone had done so much and come so far. She couldn't hurt Maria as so many others had done. She couldn't take what little hope she had away from her. We were possibly her only chance of a better life, of a new life and now it was all going to end in a few simple words. Jamie saw Inna crying and wondered over, putting his arms around her, comforting her.

"I can't tell her," Inna cried, "I just can't tell her."

Andrey came over and sat awkwardly with them. Inna completely understood Jamie's difficult position and the awkward circumstances but it was going to be so very difficult for her to tell Maria.

Andrey whispered "Let's give it a go."

After a short while sitting silently thinking, Jamie said "I have an idea."

Andrey and Inna looked up and Inna wiped the tears from her eyes. "Why don't we do this step by step? Why don't we refurbish her old legs, making them much more comfortable? In this way Maria will slowly get used to walking again and feel what it would really be like wearing comfortable sockets and Össur won't end up wasting the expensive components. We will keep these components for her so that if and when she is finally ready I will come back and replace her old legs with the new ones."

Inna jumped up and said "Oh, thank you, thank you," and kissed Jamie on the cheek. Andrey smiled. It was the answer.

The three of them went to where Maria had been sitting quietly, waiting.

"OK" Jamie said, "We will do it your way, not in a week but step by step." Maria looked up, surprised. "We will refurbish your old legs, giving you new sockets so you can feel what it will be like wearing comfortable legs. We will prove to you what we can do. I will take these components back with me to the UK but they will remain in my house and as soon as you are ready I will come back and replace your old legs with the new ones."

Maria looked at Jamie, smiled, and said "OK, let's go, what are we waiting for?"

Chapter 11

On Two Legs

They all squeezed into Andrey's car, after making a very hasty retreat from the clinic where they had attracted a bit of attention. Nurses and doctors, as well as a few patients peered through the doors to the conservatory gardens. The name Heather Mills-McCartney had quickly circulated around the staff and everyone wanted to know what was going on. Maybe many had expected that Heather was there herself. After making their excuses that they were not going to use the clinic after all, and thanked them for their help anyway – even though they didn't actually do a thing – Jamie, Andrey, Inna and Maria drove off.

Maria suddenly seemed completely different, chatting and giggling in the car as they made their way through the traffic to Andrey's workshop in the town of Reutov, about forty minutes drive from central Moscow. Andrey's workshop, the Reutov Orthopaedic Centre, was one of the best Russian workshops Jamie had seen.

There were two choices for the disabled to acquire artificial limbs in Russia – they could either go to a state run clinic or to a private clinic like Andrey's. The State pays a small amount for prosthetics for the disabled and, if a patient chooses a private clinic, the Russian Government demands that he or she presents plenty of necessary and frequently unnecessary documents supporting that choice.

However, once the bureaucracy was out of the way, Andrey could provide his patient with good limbs and eventually reclaim most of the money from the State. Andrey was in collaboration with Össur and used their products in the limbs he provided his patients, but Andrey's company wasn't a big company, he only had about five or six full-time staff – all of whom were wonderful, kind, warm-hearted caring people that Inna immediately felt comfortable with. She believed that it wasn't just because of this project that they were being particularly helpful – she felt they were like it all of the time. It seemed that they made a lot less money than many of the other private prosthetic companies in Moscow but they were humanitarianists to the end.

The workshop was situated close to the centre of the town. It looked like an old shop. Andrey had downstairs while another company rented upstairs. They entered through the main doors, through a small showroom displaying prosthetic components and into the workshop and offices.

Jamie had already briefed Andrey as to what he would need and everything was ready. Andrey had invited a few colleagues to watch and understand how Jamie assembled the components and made the sockets and legs. Although the end result was more or less the same, it was extremely interesting for the Russian prosthetists to see how a Western prosthetist worked – they would swap notes and ideas and discuss procedures. Andrey asked whether he could film Jamie working. Maria didn't mind. Maria was very happy – she was now the centre of attention and was enjoying every minute. Jamie talked and Inna was kept busy translating questions and answers as the Russians looked on and took notes. The Icecross silicone liners were fitted and casts taken of both of Maria's residual limbs. This was quite difficult for Maria as she had to be supported on a plinth with the limb that needed to be cast hanging over the edge. Maria was not very comfortable, but she had changed completely from the Maria they saw that morning, she put up with the awkwardness and discomfort and remained giggly and cheerful, joking with everyone grouped around watching. At the end of that very difficult and quite traumatic day two good casts had been produced. The day had passed quickly and, after a few last questions, they wrapped everything up at about six in the evening. They were all tired, but a start had been made – the first important step.

Maria was told she wouldn't be needed the following day, as most of the work would be in the workshop working on the casts and sockets. Maria had taken a week off from the streets and was pleased that she could spend the day with her son who was staying with Lydmilla. Maria arranged to meet Anton and Lydmilla back at her room in Lunevo. Andrey arranged with a driver to take her back to the train station and they all kissed and hugged as she left.

That evening Jamie took Inna to dinner at a small restaurant opposite the Moscow

Tchaikovsky Conservatory. As they sat and ate and discussed the day, they watched as Muscovites filed past the pillared entrance into one of the popular concert halls in Russia. Founded in 1866 by world famous pianist and conductor Nikolay Rubinstein, the Moscow Conservatory, with over one thousand undergraduate students, is said to be one of the finest and most famous schools of music in the world.

It was a great end to a great day. Jamie settled the bill. Inna felt guilt but there was nothing she could do. She had no money, certainly not enough to eat out and Heather had refused to pay any of their expenses, so Jamie paid from his own pocket that night and throughout the rest of that week. Inna saw Jamie back to Olga's apartment and then took the Metro and minibus all the way back to

Zelenograd, finally getting to bed, totally exhausted, just after one am.

Five hours later her alarm rang and she struggled out of bed and back to Jamie's apartment. Inna knew Moscow and understood what could happen to foreigners – how easily they are targeted by both police and criminals. She also knew how difficult travelling on the Metro can be for someone that spoke no Russian. Although Jamie had travelled the world she felt responsible for him while he was in Moscow and so made sure she met him at his apartment every morning and made sure he got back to the apartment safely every night. He later said to her that she would make a good mother, always protective and caring and aware of what could happen.

They then caught the yellow Metro line to Novogireevo, at the very end of the line, where Andrey met them and drove them to Reutov. That day Inna spent translating backwards and forwards between Jamie, Andrey and the rest of the team. As Jamie started work on Maria's legs, the degree of hip flexion contractures and spinal curving became more apparent. Because Maria had spent many years on her wooden platform, the residue limbs had set at an angle of thirty degrees, which meant she could not, in fact, straighten her legs from the pelvis. This was greater than they had originally thought. The team, along with a medical doctor, sat down and discussed what could be done. This was going to be tricky as a thirty degree angle was one of the biggest they had come across. They decided to compromise with a fifteen degree alignment which would give Maria just enough hip flexion to be comfortable while reducing the strain on her lower back. At fifteen degrees the cosmetic shape of the prosthetic would also be maintained. They filled the plaster models at that degree of flexion and carried out the required modification. Before proceeding to the definitive sockets, transparent sockets were used to allow confirmation of the socket fit and to assess comfort. Although Inna's voice was becoming hoarser by the minute, surprisingly everything was all going to plan and the legs were slowly taking shape.

Andrey's driver picked Maria up at nine am on day three. She was cheerful and worked happily with Jamie and Andrey as they fitted the left and right sockets. A small weight-bearing jig was set up and Maria was carefully placed onto it to assess comfort and fit of the two sockets. At first each socket was tested individually, and then both together. Maria was told that because these sockets were completely new they will feel different and unusual and so it was vitally important for Jamie to have constant feedback from Maria, and Maria worked hard responding on her feelings of comfort and sensations. After initial difficulty with the left limb, both sockets were eventually shown to be a good fit, in terms of comfort and control, although further slight adjustments would probably still be needed prior to the manufacture of the definitive sockets. Jamie finally showed Maria his prosthetic.

"I want one just like that," she said.

"You will have." he replied. Maria was back to her normal self, charming everyone around her.

For Andrey and Jamie day four was the longest and hardest. Inna had been given the day off and Andrey had found another interpreter. Andrey spoke little English and so an interpreter was essential for them to communicate effectively and efficiently. Both of the provisional sockets were filled with plaster and the required adjustments made. To trap the moisture within the plaster models, the casts were sealed with lacquer. The casts were then draped with a soft plastic and the residual third was cut away, leaving a collar would improve sitting comfort and cosmesis. The locks were positioned and secured by the first lamination. The adapter that would connect the socket to the remainder of the limb was positioned and secured by the second lamination. The new sockets were almost ready to be connected to Maria's existing prosthetics.

At ten pm Jamie called Inna from the workshop to ask her to ask Maria to be at the station at ten am the following day. Everything was set. Tomorrow Maria would take her first proper comfortable step in almost nineteen years.

Because of the traffic Maria had been waiting outside the train station for almost an hour.

"He's coming," Inna said two or three times as she kept calling Maria telling her not to worry, that Andrey was on his way. Moscow traffic on a Friday morning is as bad as in any other major city around the world. It was a bad start to what was going to be a difficult day. Finally Andrey tooted the horn and Maria wheeled herself over to his car. Andrey jumped out and lifted Maria into the front seat throwing her platform into the back. They sped off.

Maria wore her best clothes that day, and had especially done her hair and applied a little makeup. She wanted to feel good on this eventful day. She hadn't slept much the previous night, tossing and turning and laying staring up at the ceiling wondering what was going to happen and where her life was eventually going to take her. Would she actually be walking comfortably by the end of that day? Was she really going to stand amongst the rest of the team, at their level, no longer having to look up to them and them looking down at her?

Finally, and almost two hours late, Andrey arrived at the workshop. That morning both sockets were trimmed and prepared for the final fitting. The new sockets were different to Maria's old sockets – they would be a lot more comfortable. More modern techniques of manufacture were now being used since her old sockets were originally made in Russia a few years earlier. Also, the material differed slightly

as a soft plastic was now going to be included in the manufacturing process. This was because, in Maria's case, a lot of
the time would be spent sitting when wearing her new prosthetics and so sitting comfort was a focus. Plastic allows the
thigh to move a lot more freely than a non-flexible material.
However, the sockets were now bigger than her old original
sockets. Maria looked at her sockets horrified.

"I am not wearing those," she screamed. "Look what
you have done to me." Jamie and the team stood, shocked.

Jamie, with Inna translating, sat next to Maria and,
through her tears, explained that the new sockets were different because of the fifteen degrees of flexion that had
been built in to support her hip. She knew that she had a
very bad curvature of the spine and these new sockets
would help prevent it getting worse. If she continued on her
platform her spine would eventually disintegrate. Then she
would be unable to go anywhere or do anything, she would
be paralyzed. Jamie said that her long term health was
more important than the size of the sockets, and anyway,
he said, she hasn't tried them on yet.

"But they look horrible," she cried. Maria wanted to
look good and she couldn't see beyond the initial outward
appearance of the new sockets. "I am not wearing them."
Like many people with diseases or illnesses they somehow
felt they knew more about their illness than the doctors
treating them, Maria felt the same. She had been disabled
almost all her life and felt that she knew what was best for
her and her condition.

"All right," Andrey said, "We will leave you here for a
while on your own. You can play around with the components. Try them on, see how you feel."

Jamie, Andrey and Inna left the room and went across
the hallway to the kitchenette and made themselves some
tea. A few minutes later the door burst open and Maria
wheeled herself in crying hysterically. She couldn't even put

them on – the whole week was a waste. She will never trust anyone again. Everything was a waste.

Jamie and Inna stood and watched as Andrey ushered Maria back into the room from where she came, looking down at the sockets and components discarded and scattered on the floor. Inna and Jamie sat silently in the kitchenette, sipping tea, not knowing what to do or what to say, listening to the hysterical sobs of Maria in the other room. Slowly the sobs dissolved and then there was silence. They sat looking at each other.

"Guys," Andrey called "Come here."

Inna and Jamie jumped up and rushed across the hall and into the room. Maria stood there, smiling.

The new sockets were amazing. They fitted perfectly. Jamie took a mirror and walked around Maria as she looked at herself at every angle. There was no apparent ugly rim – it was impossible to see that she had artificial legs under the short skirt she was wearing. She giggled and laughed like a child who at first rejects something and then realizes what they initially rejected was actually quite wonderful. Maria was a child, but a child they had all come to love.

Supporting herself with full-length crutches she slowly got used to her new legs. She was walking comfortably for the first time in her life. Amazingly, after ten or fifteen minutes walking around the workshop, she asked for shorter elbow crutches. Jamie and Andrey were uncertain, saying it was far too early, but she insisted. They reluctantly handed her a pair and watched nervously as she gingerly supported herself and slowly started to walk. It was unbelievable.

The week was coming to an end. Jamie explained the exercises and training Maria would have to do over the next few months, and then, if all goes well, Jamie would come back and fit brand new components. Maria promised.

Jamie, Inna and Andrey took Maria to the train station where her helper was waiting. They kissed and hugged and said their emotional farewells and watched Maria through the window smiling and waving as the train pulled away.

That evening they celebrated.

After a day with Jamie sightseeing, Inna flew back to the UK early Sunday morning and an exhausted Jamie returned to England Sunday afternoon.

Chapter 12

The Book

On the 5th October 2004 I wrote to Heather asking if I could interview her for the book. I wanted to talk in detail about her charity and describe the work that she had done with other disabled people around the world. I honestly and genuinely wanted to show that, despite everything, and despite what we still felt were her unfulfilled promises, there was a compassionate and caring side to Heather. I had already agreed to give half my royalties from the sale of this book to Maria and The Maria Foundation. The money would eventually go towards helping her start a new life off the streets, but I also made a promise to Heather to donate some of my royalties to her Charity. Three weeks after I had written to her she replied saying that she rarely does interviews as things are hardly ever written as discussed plus it would take up too much time she could be having with her baby. "Having said that", she said, "when a writer gives her the headline, photo and a copy for approval before publication", she does occasionally consider interviews. But, she said, the problem was Fiona, her publicist – it would be more work for her as she would have to check everything. Heather also said that because we would make little or no profit from the book the money I would donate to her charity would be irrelevant. Her book, "A Single Step", took years just to

pay off the advance. There were no royalties and her book
has now been discontinued.

So it seemed to Inna and me that Heather Mills-
McCartney just didn't want to know. We felt that all those
initial promises of helping Maria all she could meant
absolutely nothing. Heather couldn't even be bothered to
give me an hour of her time – it simply wasn't worth it to
her as, in her own words, I will make no profit from the
book and my promises of donating to her charity were
"irrelevant."

On the 2nd December 2004 I wrote to her again, asking if
she could at least write a forward to the book. In that way
Fiona would not have any "extra work" and Heather could
even write the forward sitting next to her daughter! On the
15th December, Sonya replied telling me that Heather was
up to her eyes in work and asking who the publishers were.
After I replied, on the 17th December she wrote again
saying Heather couldn't do anything until February 2005,
but if I would like to write the Forward from Heather
myself, which would have to be approved before publication. Of course I declined.

Epilogue

Maria has been working hard practicing walking, using her new legs. A few weeks ago she and Anton spent a few hours just walking around Moscow city centre. She says that one of the most amazing things she has experienced while wearing her new legs is that she can now look at people at eye level. With legs nobody stares down at her, no longer demeaning her, degrading her. She is on the same level – socially, psychologically and physically – with everyone else around her.

The next stage is that Jamie will go back to Moscow in the summer of 2005 and replace the refurbished Russian legs with new modern Össur legs. The legs will then have to have the cosmesis coverings fitted and Maria can once again strand proud amongst others around her. Heather had promised that she will pay for the cosmesis at the Dorset clinic, but we have to question whether this promise will be honored. We have started raising the money, just in case. Maria then needs to get off the streets and into a job – after so many years asking others for money, she wants to earn her own money and take Anton to places she has only dreamed about, and to buy him things that she could only see through a glass window. One day Maria will do all of these things, and more.

Commenting upon the work Inna and I had done to help Maria, a friend of ours said that we must be proud of what we had achieved. But there is nothing to be proud of; we have only helped the one person. But, he stressed, it was not just the one person, it was also Maria's son, and his children and his children's children and everyone involved in the project, and everything that has evolved from the project, and the contacts and the friends and the hopes and emotions people have experienced. A whole world has changed from one conversation over two years ago outside a dirty Metro station in Moscow. If everyone could change just one person's life, there would be no more poverty, no more hardship, no more suffering and sadness. With determination and will power we can *all* do something amazing.

We are hoping to bring Maria and Anton to the UK in the summer. We want to take them to London, and Windsor and Cambridge and show them all the wonderful things they have only seen on the television and in films. Maria also wants to meet some of the people that have shared her life over these past couple of years. She wants to personally thank them as well as to try and understand their compassion and kindness and what motivated them to help a girl they don't know living in a strange country so far away.

The day before this book went off for publication we heard from Jamie. He had just spoken to Andrey at the clinic in Moscow. Maria went there to be assessed for new sockets as her limbs have changed shape slightly since the sockets were first fitted. Andrey stood amazed as Maria walked around the clinic on her prosthetics but without any help from her crutches. He had never seen anything like it. It is virtually unheard of for someone with that kind of disability to walk unaided.

Maria is a survivor.

The Maria Foundation

Our first priority is to get Maria off the streets. Unfortunately Inna and I are not wealthy enough to personally sponsor her, nor do we want to promise her money and find later we can't afford it and have to stop, so first we are looking for a more permanent sponsor or sponsors. If we can find a promised regular amount which will give her and her son enough to live on without begging, it will then give her time and the ability to help us develop our Foundation. We will need to work with someone in Moscow and Maria is the only person that we really want to work with, as she knows the environment and situation and she desperately wants to help others like herself.

We are also looking for donations and sponsorship to help Maria and others like her obtain the things that the disabled and destitute in Russia so desperately need. We want help make their lives a little more comfortable. Donations will go towards buying hats, coats and gloves. We will bring hot soup and food to those standing in the freezing snow. We will buy pens, pencils and books for the children of the impoverished and, whenever we can, help the disabled with new, comfortable limbs as well as offering the opportunity to provide new training so they can get off the streets and back into work.

We can help change so many lives it is actually quite unbelievable.

If you feel you can help in any way please contact me at:

Robin Barratt
Unit 56, 3 Courthill House
60 Water Lane, Wilmslow
Cheshire, SK9 5AJ
England
Tel: + 44 (0) 870 240 9998
E-mail: RobinBarratt@yahoo.com
Website: www.TheMariaFoundation.com